Think Differently Insights

Craig thought that he was doing the right thing by trying to see more people. What he realized is that *he couldn't even see the people who were sitting right in front of him.* As a result of making it his intent to listen to clients and understand their concerns, needs, hopes, dreams, and fears, Craig doubled his production. Just one year after being introduced to ShiftMethods training, he had a little more than 100 percent growth.

~ Transformed grinding long hours to smart, efficient interactions.

"These are high-impact words. When I start the sales meeting with the 'my bias' statement, it changes the environment. And then I noticed a switch in their countenance, I am able to give them feedback on what they have and how it's aligned to give them results they expect. I knew that my friend was on to something brilliant, and I needed more of it. Ninety percent of what I do is the same as what I've always done. The difference is in how I listen—and the way I start and conduct the meetings…well, I guess that is a lot."

~ Phil, Increased over 37% in 9 months.

The effectivity of communication is what launched my success. It's not something you can do, get it over with, and see results right away. It requires thinking about things in different ways and building repetition into your client interactions. When you do this consistently over time, you can elevate and grow your practice to levels you never imagined. And that is what I did."

~ Don went from $400k revenue to $2.1M in revenue in four years.

Her biggest hindrance was her mind-set—she didn't think she was capable of achieving at the levels of some of the top producers. What we uncovered is that she has a skill that goes way beyond the level of her mentor. She has exceeded even his level of success.

~ Cynthia discovered how capable she was.

"If they say they are all set, who am I to disagree with their perspective?" After using ShiftMethods, he said, "This stuff just makes sense. I have been taught for twenty-one years to find or create pain, convince, sell, and always be closing, but with ShiftMethods, prospects become clients just because I am asking great questions, listening, understanding them, serving them, and giving them feedback about how their assets are aligned with what is most important to them. It is much easier than I thought."

~ Matt, revolutionizes his practice.

"It is impossible to properly understand how it changes the dynamic without studying the video. ShiftMethods concepts are so new and different to advisors, they have to watch the videos to fully understand how to implement them into their process."

~ Scott, content curator.

Skepticism is healthy. If you feel skeptical right now, like Phil was at first, and you're thinking, "Yeah, right, I'm not sure I believe it…this kind of sounds too good to be true," then you're in the right place. Keep reading and pondering to unlock the star in you and help your clients see how diligent, able, and referable you are.

~ G. Wells, author

Think Differently

Think Differently

ELEVATE AND GROW YOUR FINANCIAL SERVICES PRACTICE

See LESS people, Do MORE Business.

George Wells

© 2017 by George Wells. All rights reserved.

ISBN: 1976448654
ISBN 13: 9781976448652

Table of Contents

Introduction ·ix

Chapter 1 Transform Every New Interview with "My Bias" · 1

Chapter 2 The Client Interview: A Mutual Discovery Process · 11

Chapter 3 Nine Ways ShiftMethods Advisors Are Different · 39

Chapter 4 What Do Savers Really Want? · · · · · · · · · · · · · · · · 57

Chapter 5 Our Role: To Listen and Understand · · · · · · · · · · 75

Chapter 6 How Top Producers Elevate and Grow Their Practices · 85

Chapter 7 Nine Barriers to Avoid · 93

Chapter 8 Thirteen Ways to Earn More Business
           in Less Time 101

Chapter 9 The Seven Tenets of ShiftMethods 119

           Commencement—You Deserve the Best 129

           About the Author and ShiftMethods 131

Introduction

Whether you've been in the financial services business for thirty years or are just getting started, ShiftMethods® will change your life. What if you could have your clients talking about you with the same excitement they exhibit when talking about new electronic gadgets? Well, not only is it possible, it *will* happen using the ShiftMethods process.

Over the past decade, ShiftMethods has been refined to be the most effective blend of strategy, training, and process. Can you envision:

1. Improving your introduction-to-close ratio by 50 percent?
2. Increasing your case size by 50 percent?
3. Transforming your business into 100 percent referrals, no longer spending your time, effort, and resources "looking" for clients, and finding people already excited about you before you meet?
4. Reducing your time in the office by 50 percent?
5. Creating such powerful positioning in your market that you eliminate your competition?

The goal of the ShiftMethods team is to enlighten and inspire your awareness of what is possible. Every giant step forward starts with awareness and vision—and thinking differently. As you merely think about ShiftMethods, you will see a change in your perspective and a change in your productivity. Even as successful as you likely already are, as you progress, you will elevate your practice to yet another level in sales effectivity and increase your skills in a way that benefits both savers (your prospects and clients) and, of course, you! You will experience the following:

- Greater effectivity
- Greater success
- Greater enjoyment

I observe traditional sales as a "predator vs. prey" model. Too often, financial advisors are taught to attempt to "drive a wedge" between a saver and his or her current advisor or financial plan and attempt to convince prospects that their own products are the best without taking time or interest to determine what is most important to the clients and what is *good* about their current plan. This results in a big missed opportunity.

Sell, sell, sell...ABC—*Always Be Closing*. We've seen countless movies highlighting the behind-the-scenes hustle of manipulative and borderline-deceitful techniques rumored to be taught to financial reps to sell products.

And you know what? It doesn't have to be that way!

ShiftMethods training is for financial professionals seeking to elevate their client interaction experience. If you're a client reading this book, it's a great opportunity to "look behind the scenes" and see the motivations, methods, and techniques the elite financial professionals use.

Serving vs. Helping

With all the chaos and complexity in the financial markets, it's more important than ever to understand our clients and prospects to serve them better.

We prefer to use the word "serve" as opposed to "help." The concept of "helping" assumes that one person is in a subordinate position to another. But "serving" assumes that both people have equal status. The advisor and the client are on the same side of the table. This creates a partnership in which both parties are working together toward the same goals. Your professional skills will be elevated and valued because your methods foster insight, empathy, and advocacy.

This is opposite what has been typical over the years in the financial service business—the information-harboring, uptight, dark-suit-wearing advisor sitting behind a mahogany desk, dictating recommendations in a somewhat condescending "father knows best" tone. No one ever liked this approach, and in the age we live in today, few savers tolerate it. The most sought-after clients want to be served by a professional they can relate to who makes financial matters simple and clearly cares about their best interest. In summary, we serve well.

> "Serving well is living well. As you are giving, you will be receiving. What you have, achieve, and enjoy is a multiplied measure of what you give."
>
> —*George Wells*

Here's a Challenge

Can you envision giving yourself to success? We experience the adage, "What you have, achieve, and enjoy is a multiplied measure of what you give." This does not make sense mathematically. How could one give up something yet receive a multiplication in return? It does not make sense logically, yet naturally it always works.

Think of a time when you were young and some teacher, mentor, or other caring elder took time to invest in you. That person may have noticed something positive about you that others overlooked. Or maybe he or she encouraged you or taught you something you never forgot.

What often creates the impact is the fact that someone saw you, heard you, and did something to leave a positive impact that you never forgot. With ShiftMethods, you are creating those "moments of impact" in every meeting. You are leveraging your role as a highly skilled financial professional with a higher level of impact, being known and experienced as a lifelong, key person of impact. Ideally, our clients look back on the day they met you as a key transition in their saving careers.

Financial professionals are often underappreciated, which unfortunately often results in clients being underserved. Typically, financial professionals are known by the "products they sell." If an advisor is well liked, the clients will say to others, "Hey, you should talk to my guy. He got me this special investment…" That is flattering, but everyone has different needs. An investment that is ideal for one saver might not be recommended for another.

What if a friend referred you to her physician, and she is excited because he put her on a special drug called Lysikstratton?

THINK DIFFERENTLY

You may be thinking, "I don't need Lysikstratton!" The drug worked great for your friend because she has a specific medical condition. But you don't think you have the same issue. You may think, "I don't need that prescription, so I don't need to see your doctor—regardless of how great the medication is for you."

ShiftMethods advisors are known by the *experiences they create* (rather than the financial tools they prescribe) in facilitating a discovery process that encourages savers to align financial resources with what is most important to them. Our clients tell their friends, family members, and others, "Wow, you've got to meet my financial advisor. I've never met anyone like him/her."

It is possible that someone who is referred to you believes they are "all set" and don't need your services. It's like the patient who hates prescriptions—he probably doesn't want to take any medications, but he would be happy to be referred to a highly recommended physician to hopefully confirm that he is fit as a fiddle. As the doctor goes through the process of discovery, it creates a great experience for that patient. Even if nothing is wrong, the patient is likely to refer that doctor to people he knows because he had a positive and insightful experience.

When you are at your best, you are the financial hero for your clients! Successful advisors I meet are on the perpetual prowl to improve their practices and will go to any length to be the best. They embody the entrepreneurial quest and take little for granted. I believe entrepreneurs are the future of humanity. They're the ones who are driving human progress, creating jobs, and building real value in the world. And that's one of the reasons I'm so passionate about our business—it's all about serving people. Service at its core is giving for the sake of doing what is right for the recipient and trusting the principle of reciprocity.

Giving is the key. I challenge you to give more than you ever have before. I challenge you to be the best version of you. Seeking to be just like others will limit you in the end. Be the best version of yourself. Step back and look at your practice. Is something missing? Is there room for something better, or something more? Is it possible for you to be more efficient, more fulfilled, or more successful in the way you define success? You are likely thinking, "I can always get better; that's why I'm reading this book."

Here's the good news: we are living in the greatest time in human history. More retirees are living longer, healthier, and more prosperous lives than ever before. Their opportunity is to "retire happily ever after," and our privilege is to show them how.

ShiftMethods training is a process of transforming a seller's mind-set from *convincing people to buy* to *facilitating alignment of people's plans with their expectations and most importantly, hopefully avoiding regret*. Your life will never be the same.

Warning, Advisors!

Many advisors are looking for the quick fix, the silver bullet. They want to find a solution and get it over with quickly. But learning to shift your approach takes time. Not because the tools are so complex, but rather because the habits you made and that have become entrenched so deeply are quite difficult to modify. The initial response from many advisors who use ShiftMethods is, "It just makes sense...yet implementation is more complicated than it seems at first." You must stay committed to it and consistent with it to see the results you hope to achieve.

Let's look at how the ShiftMethods process works and what makes it so effective in building trust and long-term relationships with prospects and clients.

Change Is Disruptive...Instead, Keep What's Working

ShiftMethods does not replace the strategies that are working for you now; they simply enhance your interaction effectivity. They enable you to shift into even more success than you're already experiencing.

We know change is disruptive. But what's even more disruptive is the feeling of regret of your future self failing to continue to improve and missing the opportunity to build a better practice and better client relationships...feeling the regret of what you could have achieved if you had learned the techniques earlier. As my grandfather, Leo Sonnenberg, always said, "You can't learn it any younger!"

This is not to suggest that you are somehow way off course and missing the boat. We find that most advisors tend to underestimate the value of the processes they're currently using.

You read that correctly—they underestimate the value of their current processes.

When I work with advisors to integrate ShiftMethods into their current processes, typically 90 percent of what they do is quite effective. We start from where you are.

To make this book most beneficial for you, assess how each of the ShiftMethods strategies is different from or similar to what you are currently doing. You may say something like, "Well, that's pretty much what I do." Ask yourself, "If I were going to approach the process *exactly* the way ShiftMethods does it, how would I change my current methods, and what would it look like?" Thinking differently is where progress begins.

How the ShiftMethods Process Was Born

Do you remember your very first closing opportunity in this business? Well, my first opportunity seemed like a total disaster, but in the months to follow, it proved to be a life-changing event.

When I made the move from engineering to the financial services world, to attempt to look the part, I bought a seven-year-old 1999 Cadillac STS Seville for $9,600. It had quite a few miles, and the seller somehow masked the revolting smell of smoke that soon emerged, but it still looked great. I needed an appropriate vehicle because I was going to meet with people in their homes.

Back then, I would send out postcards to people who were looking for information about estate planning, tax planning, or the "recent government changes." Then I would talk to them about their investments, in hopes of finding some retirement assets that needed attention. I was taught that the goal was to drive a wedge between them and their current plan.

Here's the scene…

It was the night before my very first closing opportunity. I was so nervous and apprehensive that I couldn't sleep. This was my big debut. The couple had set up an estate plan based on a previous meeting we had, and I was going to help fund the trust. I had had some training, but in hindsight, I realized it was the "predator vs. prey" type of training. I started going through what I was taught. I asked him, "Did your broker ever tell you this? Why do you have these investments?" I was beginning to attempt to "drive the wedge."

And then the client told me something that made me stop. He said, "I don't know if it makes any difference, but we're planning on purchasing a home up north in the next six to twelve months, and we want your advice on how we should manage our investments."

With my training, I probably should have said, "Well, we can set aside some money to put a down payment on the property and then finance the rest of the purchase." But they were getting ready to *build* a home. My experience with building and rehabbing homes had taught me that it's hard to know just how much cash a person is going to need in that situation. So the best advice I could give them, even though it was contrary to what I had been taught, was that they should probably liquidate their nonqualified investments, put the money in the bank, and see how much money they would need. Then maybe we could talk in the future about investing some of it.

The couple had not saved a significant amount of money for retirement. In their case, with their plans of building a home, although it could be easily justified, to me it didn't make sense for them to redeploy their assets into investments where I could make money. Little did I know that this disruption in what I was taught was the beginning of what we know today as ShiftMethods. Even though it looked like it was not going well for me, it ended up turning out great. I finished going through the process with the clients as we went through the estate plan and got everything in order, as promised.

Afterward, they said, "We appreciate this so much. Thank you for what you've done. Now, how do we pay you?"

I replied, "Well, I set up the plan and implemented it for you. I got things in order for you, and that's really how I'm compensated."

We both knew I wasn't going to get paid anything. About three weeks later, the client called me and said, "George, dear friends of ours from church would like to meet with you. They have some questions about their retirement savings."

My assumption was that "birds of a feather flock together" and that I would find this new couple in a similar financial situation as their friends. Nevertheless, I was very thankful for the opportunity and eager (nearly desperate) to see whoever I could.

Once I met with them, I was surprised to learn they had several hundred thousand dollars of retirement assets. Now, there I was brand new in my career, meeting with a couple who had (what seemed like) quite a nest egg (for a beginner). And based on their friends' experiences, I had come highly recommended because their friends saw me as one who did the right thing, even though I was new in the financial business. In the end, I put together a plan for them, and it was one of my first cases I ever closed. It was huge because of what is now labeled "ShiftMethods thinking."

With that first closing opportunity, I didn't do what I had been told. I didn't do what I was taught. I did what I felt was right. I just tried to be there for them and *with* them, and you know what? Reciprocity has its way of coming right back to you. That is where the ShiftMethods process was born—listening, being attentive, being patient, what I would later learn to be called "building empathic connection," and most importantly, doing the right thing for the client. That means developing a strategy that's clearly in *their* best interest—not thinking about immediate gratification but thinking about what my reputation would be in the long term. If I tried to grab this and grab that, I'm not sure I would have been referred to their friends. More importantly, I'm quite sure I would not be writing this today. But because they saw I was trying to do best for them, they had good reason (based on our encounter) to trust me and send others to me.

It was an amazing experience I had immediately in my career that's continued to feed itself over and over and over again. One day, I was losing sleep, feeling the pressure of trying to close business based on what I was taught. The next day, I left my first big-deal appointment feeling let down and a little embarrassed that I didn't "sell any financial products" because I went in there and tried to do the best thing for people. Then a few weeks later, I was referred to a case that completely exceeded my expectation. Now, that is a story with a great ending! And fortunately, as time has passed, we've been writing the script for many, many stories like this, impacting thousands of savers.

About This Book

Over the years, I've gotten the nickname "financial protagonist" because I've refashioned an old script of service and made it new and progressive. I enjoy facilitating savers' ability to retire happily ever after by really listening to them share their hopes, dreams, and fears. In addition to working with financial advisors to build their practices, I am still a personal producer. I believe it's important to stay relevant and to continue to experience the same challenges every financial advisor faces every day.

Everything you will learn here—in this book, on the website, and through the training program—is based on results I experience personally in my own practice every day. I created this formula through massive amounts of what I like to refer to as "self-inflicted training"—trial and error, testing, and hard-won experience. I've invested more than $250,000 in training, mentorship, and coursework. With each new idea or method, I test, modify, test, refine, and then modify, test, and refine again to see the highest mutual benefit before passing the method on to our great advisors.

I am intensely passionate about my most valued asset—time. The reason I wrote this book is to do once (create videos and write this material) what many thousands will be able to enjoy over and over and over again. My goal is to impact millions of people and affect more than $1 trillion of savings. I hate wasting time. Every chapter in this book should either reinforce something you've heard before, bring clarity, teach you something new, or enable you to take something away that you can apply immediately. By supplementing what you're already doing with some proven methods, you can improve every aspect of your practice—and your life.

Now, let's look at how the ShiftMethods process works—and what makes it uniquely effective.

CHAPTER 1

Transform Every New Interview with "My Bias"

With all the chaos and complexity in the financial markets, it is more important than ever to connect with clients and prospects in a way that serves them. The optimum way to begin a client interview (which many financial advisors call a "sales meeting") is to begin with what I call the "bias statement." This early commitment is a great key to improving your ability to build trust and rapport with clients and increase your Assets Under Management.

Begin Every Interview Like This

When I meet someone for the first time, I tell them "my bias" early in the interview. This sets the tone of expectation for the meeting. Here is a story of Mr. and Mrs. Griffin, who were referred to me by their neighbor, Sheila. Here's what I say:

> Mr. and Mrs. Griffin, I believe everyone has a bias. I want to share with you what my bias is: My bias is that you would

have an experience meeting and working with me that would exceed your expectation so much that you will go back to Sheila, the one who referred you, and thank her for referring you to me. Whether we have any reason to do business together or not, my bias is that your experience would be a positive reflection on your relationship with Sheila, and you would be grateful she referred you to our office.

So, if I do or say anything during any of the time we spend together that rubs you the wrong way or doesn't seem quite right, I want you to stop me immediately and make me aware of it. Does that make sense?

Beginning your meeting this way has a multiplicity effect. Here are four of the most significant benefits:

1. Not only do you set the expectation that you will have served your prospects well, but you are having them serve you by giving you feedback.
2. This introduction will completely shift the energy in the room. Instead of savers coming in thinking they are going to "kick the tires" and see what you offer, you are now talking to them in a way that engages them in conversation.
3. Knowing you want them to benefit from your time together, they will likely give you more information. That is indeed the goal—for them to benefit from their meeting with you and to get their expectations met. The only way for that to happen is for them to fully engage with you. The only way for them to fully engage with you is for you to create an atmosphere of serving. They must know you are there to benefit them, first and foremost.

4. When sitting with clients for the first time, this conversation shifts their perspective so they feel that you are sitting on the same side of the table as they are and that you are truly there to listen to them well and serve them well.

Advisors tell me it is beneficial for them to watch the "bias" video many times to get the conversation right when they meet with clients. It takes practice, either by yourself or with colleagues. Not only are you changing what you say, more importantly, you are modifying your mind-set. This is monumental.

In some ways, ShiftMethods is a new and awkwardly different approach to something you've done for a long time.

It can feel like riding a two-wheel bike, but...backwards. Just about everyone knows how to ride a two-wheel bike. But then we tell them, "OK, that's great. Now sit your bottom on the front handlebars and ride the bike backwards." It's the same concept. It's just balance and peddling, but everything is in reverse. They're thinking, "Riding forward has always worked well for me. How could anyone benefit any more from riding backwards?" And that's how it can feel to shift the focus of your client interview.

Advisors will say, "I pretty much do that with my clients already." In athletics, pretty much scoring is *not scoring*. If you are not doing it exactly, you are not doing ShiftMethods. Don't feel bad. As humans, we have an inherent need to feel right, so we resist admitting that a slight shift in the way we do things may result in a better outcome. I know this isn't you, right? After all, you are reading the book. You've already set yourself apart as a striver who wants to be the best. At first, people tend to think these are "just words." But the nuances are important. The nuances are the difference between catapulting your practice or settling for your own level of mediocrity. You have good reason to fear mediocrity. It will keep you from greatness if you let it.

> *"Mediocrity is always nipping at the heels of the great."*
> —George Wells

Have you ever gone into the home of someone who has one of those little "yapper dogs"? They weigh about thirteen pounds, have a little raspy bark, and won't stop barking until you sit down. Then when you try to get up and go somewhere, they start that raspy barking again and nip at your pants leg or your heels. As long as you're not moving, there is peace, but as soon as you try to get up and do something, the little dog gets all bent out of shape and tries to discourage you by nipping at your heels. He wants you to sit back down and do nothing.

Greatness is not an accident.

Imagine what it takes to be awarded the top prize in a bake-off. When you're baking a cake, it just turns out better if you are super particular about the process. What seems like a meaningless nuance can actually be a game changer. What's the difference between the one who bakes a cake that tastes good and the one who takes the top prize at the state fair? I don't know, but the judges can tell the difference. Our clients are the judges. When you are the best version of yourself, your greatness comes out. And you will get the grand prize.

Phil, a Former Skeptic, Shifts Methods and Transforms His Client Interactions

One of my advisor clients who had been using ShiftMethods very successfully for a while referred one of his friends named Phil,

THINK DIFFERENTLY

who was a successful advisor. And, like many successful advisors who have experimented with many different sales training programs, he was open but also a serious skeptic. Phil asked a lot of questions about how ShiftMethods can make a difference in a successful person's practice. I told him, "The real difference is that your clients feel like you're sitting on the same side of the table as them, and it facilitates an environment in which they want to do business with *you*, almost without exception."

His response was, "Yeah, right. Is there anything you can show me? Is there anything you can give me that I can try?"

I gave Phil a few videos; one of them was the "my bias" video that describes the interview-opening approach you just read about. He told me, "I'm going to do this based on the recommendation from my buddy, basically to prove it wrong. A friend of mine swears by it, but I can't believe just saying those words can make any difference. They're just words. But I'm going to use the bias opening with ten people and see if it makes any difference."

He did use the opening with his clients, and after about three weeks, he called me to tell me he wanted to apply to be part of the training. Apparently, he saw a glimpse of what his friend had been experiencing. With just a few videos, Phil experienced value. I teased him, saying, "Why? They're just words."

"These are high-impact words," he said. "When I start the sales meeting with the 'my bias' statement, it changes the environment. People are opening up to me who wouldn't normally open up to me. They're giving me information they wouldn't normally give me. I have always wanted people to feel comfortable, but now I realize that the techniques I used in the past

5

didn't make every person feel comfortable. It made some of them feel *sold*."

Phil went on to say that using the bias statement in his client meetings, or interviews, has made a significant difference. He told the story of how a man and his wife came into his office. "The man was very standoffish, harsh, and asked a lot of hard questions (the typical strong version of the type A personality) until I noted the bias statement," Phil said. "And then I noticed a switch in his countenance. It literally felt like we moved from sitting across the table from each other, sparring as potential adversaries, to sitting on the same side of the table, partnering so that I could be of benefit to him and his wife. It was as if we were working together on the same team. I was able to give him feedback on what he has and how it's aligned to give him results he expected."

Phil explained that in the past, this would have been the type of person who would have questioned and questioned and questioned him until he found a weak spot in Phil's presentation. "The meeting might have lasted a long time, but it would have been very difficult to do business with him," Phil says. "This time, this type of person was open with me. He shared with me. He told me what his challenges were, what his fears were, and he discussed all his assets. And of course, he ended up being my client. That experience was the tipping point for me. I knew that my friend was on to something brilliant, and I needed more of it."

Phil applied on the spot for the ShiftMethods program. Now he has been using the program for almost a year. He recently told me, "Ninety percent of what I do is the same as what I've always done. The difference is in how I listen—and the way I start and conduct the meetings…well, I guess that is a lot. These techniques set the tone for everything. Using them creates a much

THINK DIFFERENTLY

more comfortable environment with prospects. I've increased my business by thirty-seven percent."

Phil added that in his first four months of using ShiftMethods, he paid for his three years of tuition more than two times over with the increase in revenue from his enlightenment.

"In the past, that type A person I mentioned may have ended up being my client, but he would have always needed to feel like he was in charge and would have been difficult for my staff and me. Using my newfound methods, I am able to find mutually beneficial ways of working with the stronger, more domineering personality types, who typically have more assets. They value my services because they see that I'm trying to serve them in how I set the tone of the interview using ShiftMethods."

(This is where you might expect to see a disclaimer such as, "Individual results may vary. If you have a heart condition, consult your physician before…" In this case, individual results will vary, and if you are like the many, many professionals who have begun to implement ShiftMethods, the biggest regret you will have is not starting earlier in your career.)

As I was writing this book, Scott from Washington gave me feedback about introducing the "My Bias" statement as text only. He said the text description misses the true benefit. "In the video, the way you use your hands, your facial expressions, and your speech intonation are very important factors that create the impact of stating your bias," Scott said. "It is impossible to properly understand how it changes the dynamic without studying the video. ShiftMethods concepts are so new and different to advisors, they have to watch the videos to fully understand how to implement them into their process."

Skepticism is healthy.

Back to Phil...if you feel skeptical right now, like Phil was at first, and you're thinking, "Yeah, right, I'm not sure I believe it... this kind of sounds too good to be true," then you're in the right place. Keep reading and pondering to unlock the star in you and help your clients see how diligent, able, and referable you are.

Those who find great success are desperate to find new ways to make it happen.

Your future is bigger than you can imagine right now. The process creates an environment in which people are thrilled with the experience they have working with you, and they refer everyone they know to you. Imagine the possibilities!

Shifting Your Methods

1. *Do not* revise the "bias statement" on the first page of this chapter so it sounds like you—say it exactly as stated at the beginning of this chapter. (After you have used it perfectly with ten prospects, you can modify it if you really think it will be better.)
2. Practice your bias statement by yourself or with someone else until you know it by heart and you are completely comfortable with it.
3. Use it with every client you meet with.
4. Evaluate how the bias statement changes the tone of your meetings and how it facilitates building relationships, understanding savers' needs, and closing sales.

Since the original writing of this book, we have had quite a number of people wanting to initiate the process for ShiftMethods while they are reading. To begin your journey, go to www.shiftmethods.com/go.

CHAPTER 2

The Client Interview: A Mutual Discovery Process

As the interviewer, your role is to take savers on a journey of mutual discovery to determine what's most important to them, discover exactly what they have, and give them feedback on what they have and how it is aligned with their expectations going forward.

As you are going through the interview process, be patient and adaptable. Keep in mind, it is very important to get through a complete interview, but the pace and time spent on each topic will be determined by the savers, your chemistry with them, and the areas that are most important to them.

We compare this interaction to visiting the public zoo with a tour guide. Imagine the life of a tour guide. Some days, the guide spends more time at the giraffe exhibit because the giraffes are out. Sometimes she spends more time at the rhinoceros exhibit because the rhinos are out. And sometimes she spends very little time at the wolf exhibit because there's not a wolf to be seen. Your interaction with your client is like traveling through every exhibit at the zoo (your fact finder). You cover every bit of material by asking every core question. And just like being at the zoo, depending on which animals are of interest, the amount of time you spend on each particular topic will be determined by the saver's level of interest and the information you gather on each topic.

When traveling through the zoo with the tour guide, we seek activity and action, which will then determine our interest level and the amount of time we spend seeing those particular animals. As this relates to the interview, we are seeking to understand and facilitate the mutual discovery process for savers to determine what is most important to them in this time frame of life.

To learn more about our mutual discovery process, go to www.shiftmethods.com/tourguide.

Sales Isn't "Sales"

Our ShiftMethods team members call financial sales professionals "facilitators." This is because the sales process, at its core, is merely facilitating clients getting what is best for them, in the most comfortable manner, with the least probability of regret. This is a different way of thinking about our role with savers. The labels of "advisor," "wealth manager," "representative," and "broker" tend to minimize the role of understanding what the saver needs, desires, and prefers. Facilitating the future success of the saver is a very high calling. It can be argued that our role is one of the most significant in society. Financial and economic instability is one of the leading causes of stress in households and can contribute greatly to relationship issues. And you know what? With the assistance of a skilled and compassionate facilitator…it doesn't have to be that way!

What We Strive to Do Exceptionally Well

As financial facilitators, we facilitate mutual discovery of the saver's concerns, history, desires, needs, preferences, fears, and expectations in a way that leaves him or her feeling listened to, understood, empathized with, and encouraged.

Here's a big, deal-breaking mistake that advisors can make: jumping to conclusions. Because we believe so strongly in our solutions, we often believe every prospect should have a portion of our product. Although that may be true, if clients have not discovered it themselves, they will not see it as a benefit. In fact, they may see your proposal as a commodity, something that makes them feel "sold." In other words, even though there is a high probability of you knowing where the conversation is going, you must be patient with savers as they discover their needs, preferences, and tendencies for themselves. As financial advisors, we all have a great responsibility to be *facilitators* of our prospects' and clients' discovery process.

Your high calling is acting as the guide/facilitator to their own self-discovery.

Don't invite them to your conclusion. Rather, invite them to their own mysteries on your journey together.

The more you see your role as a facilitator of discovery, the more successful, happy, and productive you will be. And your clients will value you deeply. Have you ever met someone who seems like a know-it-all? Always quick to give answers and slow to listen? How does it make you feel to be interacting with a know-it-all? And we all know people who are great listeners. Often, they get the label "best friend" because they listen with genuine interest.

Your role as the professional is to facilitate savers' discovery of what may or may not be of benefit to them.

In some cases, you may not be able to be of benefit. Coincidentally, a saver may have a fantastic plan that suits his or her disposition, but it has not performed well because of recent market conditions. Sometimes savers have a strategy that has done well because of market conditions. You know, based on your experience in seeing the types of investments they have, that the seemingly good plan will likely disappoint in the future. Not because of the upside potential, which they have likely benefited from, but rather because of the risk of significant downside fluctuation. This is where disappointment can happen.

And you know what? It doesn't have to be that way!

Conversely, the seemingly deficient plan that hasn't necessarily yielded the performance they hoped for may prove to "get them what they expect" soon.

An appropriate strategy minimizes the potential for disappointment and maximizes the potential for efficiency and gain relative to clients' risk/reward boundaries.

You know you represent some fantastic products, and you have a wealth of knowledge in how to implement strategy. Yet your product, your strategy, is not what makes you the greatest. As you view the ShiftMethods videos, you will discover how to unleash the greatness inside you far beyond what you've already achieved.

What makes a ShiftMethods advisor great is his or her ability to facilitate mutual discovery of the saver's concerns, history, desires, needs, preferences, fears, and expectations in a way that leaves the saver feeling listened to, understood, empathized with, and encouraged.

Going through a proper interview and helping savers discover unmet needs will result in you presenting a solution that meets those needs and exceeds their expectations. Keep in mind that this is not the traditional process of causing pain and fixing pain. This is *not* the following:

- It is not you trying to show that they or their previous advisor has done something wrong.
- It is not you attempting to "drive a wedge" between them and their current advisor or plan.
- It is not you telling them about financial products that are great.

This is simply listening and facilitating a great conversation that uncovers the opportunity for you to be of benefit to them. The differences may seem subtle, but the results are significant.

Seven Questions to Ask Yourself

In each client interview, the focus is on the saver (your prospect or client). As you are beginning a relationship with a saver, be mindful of these seven questions:

1. Does an opportunity exist for you to benefit the saver in several areas?
2. Does the saver have a sufficient amount of resources for which you can create a plan that aligns with his or her objectives?

3. Is the saver you're meeting with the primary decision maker, and can he or she make decisions alone? Does he or she need to seek other counsel?
4. Is the saver able to see benefits that exceed his or her expectations? Does the financial strategy make sense to the client because it clearly puts him or her in a better position?
5. Has your client had an experience meeting and working with you that he or she would like to share with others, unprompted? Does the client want to encourage his or her friends, family, neighbors, and associates to meet with you, whether or not you ask for referrals?
6. Most importantly, is the saver someone you can envision being a pleasure to serve years down the road? It is most fun to work with those you like. Life is too short to make a long-term commitment to someone who will likely be difficult.
7. After your interview, what could you have done better in the process with the saver to make his or her experience better in terms of the interaction and the result of working together?

A Process of Qualification

"Qualification" refers to understanding savers' needs, where they're coming from, how they value their various investments, and where they expect to go in the future, financially. The client interview is an event that helps us determine how their assets are aligned to give them what they expect and highlight any discrepancies between the portfolio they have and what is most important to them.

The goal is *not* for you to tell them what's wrong with their plan or what is wrong with their advisor. The goal is for them to realize there are some areas where they could be significantly better positioned based on their disposition and to ask you to create a strategy solution. It is significantly more impactful when you're not telling them what they could be doing; rather, through mutual discovery, *they see* objectives that are not being met, and *they are asking* you to construct a strategy solution.

Your skillful facilitation will make it easier for clients to state their objectives. Their words are much more powerful than yours. When you say it, it's *sold.* When they say it, it's *gold!*

It is easy to highlight a need someone has and tell them what to do. However, it takes a careful listener/facilitator to lead savers to tell you what they need. The conclusion is the same. Whose lips speak it determines the impact.

This process is critical because it ensures that the saver feels *heard.* When a saver self-discovers a need—and requests a solution strategy—because of the questions you ask, it is perhaps the most powerful moment in the entire qualification process. In addition, by being the listener, you can accumulate the areas of opportunity so when it is time, you can present your response to each of the challenges or topics the saver has brought up in the interview process.

Savers will give you the road map to serve them well if you are patient enough to listen and understand well.

Reiterate the conversation to be sure you have heard them. Like any good listener, be aware of giving nonverbal cues of affirmation and understanding as you are listening by simply nodding your head, taking notes, and making it clear that you are "getting" them.

What if Their Concerns Seem Trivial?

In our many years of client experiences, we've seen so many times how something that seems of little significance is one of the biggest determining factors in who savers choose to serve them financially. Being an engineer, logically this does not make sense to me. But a rule of thumb is that 80 percent of the impact is caused by 20 percent of the issues. This often does not make sense—but it doesn't need to. After all, it is the client's concern, not yours. What is most important for your clients should be what is most important for you. When they feel that you see what's most important to them, they will value you and your solution that fixes the other 80 percent as well. In a nutshell, what you see as only 20 percent of the problem, they may see as 80 percent of the impact.

Here are a few examples of the relative insignificance of daily use of retirement assets—which clients tend to worry about a lot but may not be that significant in the bigger picture. Your job is to put things in perspective for them:

- Required Minimum Distribution schedule at age 70½
- Frequency of distribution: annually, semi-annually, quarterly, or monthly
- Time between wire transfer request and cash availability
- Social Security election options
- Risk of in-law claim to assets at promotion
- Liquidity of a REIT that represents less than 3 percent of total assets
- Underperformance on a low-performing stock that represents less than 3 percent of total assets
- Federal and state withholding tax election on withdrawals

Keep in mind, if it's a big deal to them, then it should be a big deal to you. Any of these situations has the potential to feel all-consuming for the saver.

Your role, first and foremost, is to understand why that area is such a concern and facilitate the solution/strategy to alleviate that concern.

Facilitate People's Discovery of What Is Important to Them

I have four young children—two girls, ten and nine, and two boys, seven and five. My children are discovering their own independence. They want to do a lot of things themselves. Yet I'm at the age where I've often experienced a more efficient way to do the things they are trying to do. But I know I must allow them to have their own discovery process, or they may not be interested in any of my solutions when they are truly in need. Interestingly, kids' creative minds often come up with strategy that is worth noting.

"I can't" is not allowed.

In our home, we do not allow the statement "I can't." However, when the feeling arises, I encourage my kids to say, "I don't know how to do that *yet*." And so it is as adults—we are often capable of so much more if we can get beyond our initial thought of "can't."

Consequently, my goal is to encourage, empathize, and elevate when interacting with my children, my wife, friends, and other financial professionals. In fact, whenever I film a video, I place a small card underneath the camera that says:

Encourage
Empathize
Elevate

As financial professionals, and people, we can be a great positive influence on others. In every interaction, we can be mindful of being encouraging to others, empathizing with their situations, and elevating their perspective.

Gather Ammunition

In the client interview, you are gathering ammunition. By "ammunition," I am talking about vital information we learn from prospects and clients about their concerns, history, desires, needs, preferences, fears, and expectations in a way that leaves the savers feeling listened to, understood, empathized with, and encouraged.

We do this so that we can benefit them. This is not ammunition *against* them; this is ammunition for you to serve savers and to build good working relationships. We do this by asking great questions, which has the extra benefit of keeping you from talking too much and maybe sounding like a know-it-all or sounding ignorant because you're talking about something that is not applicable to them. After all, as they're talking to you, you get a better understanding of them, and you won't miss something when you begin to apply what they told you to align their assets with what is most important to them.

Fast and Fragile or Slow and Steady

We have to be careful about accepting client requests too easily and moving too fast. Sometimes a new prospect meeting can seem like it is off to a quick and easy start because the savers get right to the point of what they are looking for. And of course, being helpful individuals, we tend to be quick to fix what appears to ail them. But don't be misled: it's fast and fragile or slow and steady. We should never rush the process of properly aligning a lifetime's worth of savings and financial history. Abandoning your process and moving too quickly can make the relationship fragile. Statistically, you will get better results if you stick to the process you know works.

Vocabulary and Connotation Risk

When you go to the doctor and she asks you what you want, you might reply, "I want the pain to go away!" The doctor won't pull out her prescription pad and start writing a prescription. Instead, she will check your vital signs, ask you questions, and then ask you more questions. Then she may order some lab work (analysis) to find out exactly what is going on inside you before she suggests a strategy for you to follow to "make the pain go away." And hopefully, when you follow "doctor's orders," your pain-relief experience goes even better than you had been prepared to expect. At ShiftMethods, we want our clients to have the same experience.

In chapter 4, we talk more about "connotation prejudice."

Often, people use terminology to label things they want because those are the only words they know to describe their situation. We must be determined to find out what is behind the request or comment we hear. We must take the opportunity to drill down and clearly understand exactly what the client is saying. What's the *why* behind what they're saying? What is truly most important to them? What are they trying to accomplish? This will likely be different from what they *say* they want initially.

A careful, diligent, thorough process = a solution strategy that exceeds expectation.

Gathering appropriate ammunition to properly serve the saver requires drilling down and finding out everything you can about the saver's goals, desires, dreams, fears, and concerns.

If you're not getting the results you want when you're ready to sign paperwork, it's likely because of something you've missed by not drilling down deeply enough during the interview. You know the probability of ending well is low when you initiate the close and the prospect says these things:

- "You've given me a lot to think about."
- "I would like to research some other things you said."
- "I need to talk to my CPA or attorney about this."
- "Can you give me some more information so we can study it and get back to you?"
- "Let me talk to my son in Arizona and see what he thinks about this."

What's even worse, later, you find out that they went to another advisor and ended up with a completely different plan than what they said they wanted from you. Why does this happen? Although it could have happened for many reasons, a way to prevent or at least greatly minimize this result is to be patient, thorough, and do not present the close until it is obvious they are ready. Scott from Washington says, "The ShiftMethods videos will show you plenty of cues to affirm they are comfortable and ready to proceed or indicate that you need to continue to gather information and facilitate discussion in preparation for initiating doing business together. In the past, I was sometimes talking my clients through a close, and other times I was presenting the paperwork too soon."

The ShiftMethods strategy is an art form. Knowing when it is appropriate to commence the signing of new-client paperwork is vital. If you misjudge prospects' readiness, the big risk is that they lose the privilege of being served by you because of something you overlooked, rushed, or missed. We must be careful to strike a balance between being thorough and being decisive.

Advisors often contact me, perplexed because they have lost a client to another advisor with a completely different philosophy. I believe it's because the other advisor said or did multiple things that resonated with the saver. Even if he wasn't as thorough as you could be, he said or did some things that made sense. Or, perhaps by luck, the other advisor's personality fit well with the savers. This random luck is not for you. Using ShiftMethods, you will be keen at adapting and adjusting the dialect of your approach to resonate well with savers so they feel heard and understood.

No Problem, No Request = No Sale

ShiftMethods concepts might seem subtle, but like the bias statement, they instantly change the rapport between you and your clients in a profound way and set the stage for a much more collaborative, insightful, and effective interaction.

One such concept is that it is critical to wait until a client states that he or she has a problem that needs a solution before you begin attempting to solve what you *believe* is a problem. There are two parts to this critical concept:

1. If it's not a problem for the saver, then it's not a problem.
2. If the saver has not asked you to solve the problem, then it is not your right to even think about offering a solution to the problem.

This is counseling 101.

1. No counselor is ever able to benefit any client who doesn't feel that he or she has a problem.
2. No counselor is ever able to benefit clients—even if they admit a problem—if they don't ask for help with that problem from the counselor.

If you catch yourself thinking or saying the following, let it be a warning—you are losing focus and getting off the listening track:

- "What they need to do is…"
- "What they should do is…"
- "They have this and that and don't even seem to care…"

If you're thinking like that, you're not listening to your clients. They will see you and your products as a commodity. And if you're not listening to your clients, they will not see you as a trusted advisor. They will not see you as different from other financial representatives.

Instead, they will see you as a peddler, as a salesperson, and they will feel the need to compare what you're saying to something else. They will not move forward or feel comfortable until they've had a good chance to shop and compare you with someone else—to "kick the tires" on other proposals from other financial "salespeople."

> *"The road to mediocrity is paved with great intentions and logical explanations."*
>
> —George Wells

And you know what? It doesn't have to be that way!

As you watch the ShiftMethods videos, you will see how you nearly eliminate the perception of competition because unless you are competing with a ShiftMethods advisor, no one will be tending to savers better than you.

Using ShiftMethods, they experience a facilitator who can aid them in aligning what they have with what's most important to them.

What's most powerful is the saver's lips and your ears.

If you say it, it may be *sold*...if they say it, however, it's *gold*!

Encouraging a candid discussion will move you and the saver closer to creating a solution strategy that is mutually beneficial.

Why You Shouldn't Rush the Solution

When the interview is going well because the prospect gets right to challenges he or she faces, it can be tempting to move to the close prematurely.

Nevertheless, the *close* is the only thing left to do after we've done these things:

1. Thoroughly discussed anything and everything that could be discussed financially.
2. Done a thorough analysis on current strategy.
3. Given feedback on what the saver has and how it is aligned to get what he or she expects.

4. Highlighted significant discrepancies between what they have and what is most important to them.
5. Appropriately asked "What else?" (Read about this important concept in chapter 4.)
6. Constructed a solution strategy to set the future in motion, aligning their financial resources with what is most important to them.
7. Reviewed, summarized, and again asked if there is anything else.

The close can happen only when all the information has been gathered, the saver's disposition is well understood, and there is nothing else to do. It is a risk when the interview is short because the saver may feel like you are putting the responsibility on him or her to determine if, in fact, there is a problem and if this is the best solution because it all happens too fast. It can be hard for the saver to make sense of it logically: "How could we be chatting for this abnormally short time, and you already have a solution strategy that deconstructs and reconstructs a lifetime's worth of savings and is best for me and my family?"

But when you facilitate a proper interview, thought process, and discussion, the resulting conclusion of the need for the product, if in fact it exists, is a result of discovery over time. When savers discover that they have a need, you can help them discover a solution as well. After a proper interview, the solution will often seem too good to be true. It's like the patient telling the doctor, "You mean to tell me that if I take this pill, I will feel better and get healthier? What are the side effects again? It just sounds too good to be true!" It happens every day in medicine. And it happens every day with ShiftMethods.

You will not demonstrate good critical thinking skills to the saver if you talk about a solution before you thoroughly and completely discover what the challenges are or what the opportunity is. Skepticism says, "Clearly you have not thought out the challenges deeply if you come up with a solution so quickly."

We get excited to talk about a solution that will fix a client's needs. And savers want to believe that there is some mysteriously rare, specific solution that will fix everything for them. Often, as you know, this is, in fact, the case. However, if we don't go through the proper process, our solution cannot meet all their needs because we do not know what they are. And our solution cannot seem well justified if the saver has not felt listened to. Often, we can find a strategy that does meet all the saver's needs, and it requires a methodical approach. We must ask great questions, listen, use peer stories, and get a better understanding of the saver's perspective. We must think differently about the way we interact with clients.

The Written Plan = "We'll Think About It"

Over the years, we've observed a correlation between delivering a written plan before the close and having the client go home to "think about it," never to return.

This is discussed in much more detail in the ShiftMethods library of videos. The point is, giving a written proposal in the traditional sales process results in a sense of completion—we talked, we did the analysis, and we presented a solution.

With ShiftMethods; we talked at length, we did the analysis, we highlighted an opportunity to better align assets, and we investigated options to align assets to get what clients expect. We discussed implementation before and after the solution strategy. We aligned those assets (signed new-account paperwork), and we formally constructed a plan on paper, with exact numbers to be delivered at new-account paperwork delivery.

Although the specifics of the new strategy need to be discussed in detail, if there is going to be an exchange of a detailed plan, it should happen upon delivery of the complete transition documents. One reason to wait for this is so the values can be the actual starting account values of the new plan.

Regardless of how much your financial plan makes sense to you, if the client doesn't feel good about the interaction, the plan will often go on a shelf and not get executed. Presenting a detailed plan can be a premature attempt to feel like you have been thorough—after all, there is so much detail in the plan, how can they say no? Prematurely presenting a written plan can cause you to circumvent the proper discovery process.

With ShiftMethods, the feeling of completion does not occur until the plan has been executed.

If the saver feels great about the interaction, an extravagantly detailed outline of a plan does not need to be bound in book form yet. You can just jot it down with a pen on a blank piece of paper. In other words, savers are looking for a guide, not a fortune teller. We see that these huge forecasted plans are almost always rendered inaccurate in a year or two, when the market or the some of the products' performance numbers do not respond as projected.

Facilitators and savers want the same thing. Savers want to know they have the very best financial solution strategy based on their needs, situations, and preferences. Facilitators want to have clear and thorough interviews to help determine how savers' financial strategies align with what is most important to them and their particular cases. The end result is the same for both the facilitator and the saver—they both want to reach the saver's financial goals.

For the ShiftMethods approach to work, you must have product knowledge and be financially minded. Don't take your accumulation of knowledge for granted.

Bonus
Would you like to know more about why it makes sense for prospects to respond to a great proposal with some version of the following?

- "Wow, thank you for doing all this work."
- "It was really nice meeting you!"
- "You've given me a lot to think about."
- "I will look at this and get back to you."
- "Thank you. I'll get back to you."

Go to www.ShiftMethods.com/greatproposal to learn key insights on how to avoid those responses. You'll also learn insider secrets behind doing great work *for* your clients vs. doing great work *with* your clients.

Three Phases of Working with Savers
The process of working with savers includes three phases.

Phase 1

- *Encourage* savers to continue doing what has gone well in their saving and investing approach (never bash their current plan or advisor).

- *Empathize* with savers in the challenges they've faced over the years by asking good questions and listening to understand what is important to them going forward.
- *Evaluate* how their current plan is aligned to give them the results they expect going forward.

Phase 2 (as applicable)

- *Elevate* savers' strategy to position their assets in a way that significantly increases their probability for success and, maybe more importantly, decreases their potential for disappointment.

Phase 3 (always)

- *Extend* the financial professional (facilitator) as a resource to others (referrals). The result: the saver feels served rather than sold. Savers we serve have recognized that beginning every meeting by affirming we are there to serve them is a key component of differentiation from other financial professional experiences.

The client interview is your biggest opportunity to establish a foundation of trust, rapport, and mutual respect with everyone you meet. Make the most of every minute.

Choose Your Clients Carefully: Happy Clients = Happy Life

Being the professional you are, it is 100 percent OK for you to be particular about whom you agree to serve. When I was in engineering at Chrysler, I worked with some great people in small groups. Often, I liked working with almost everyone, but sometimes there were a couple of people who made it difficult for the rest of us to work well together, and it seemed the group may be more fun if those difficult people worked in another group.

When I entered the financial services business and started my practice, it was very important for me to be able to work only with people I thought were going to be fun to work with for the rest of their lives. Keeping that in mind has made my practice a lot more enjoyable for me, for my clients, and for my staff.

We have the privilege of being able to pick whom we work with, and we should not take that lightly. When you work with people you like, it's a happy life—for you and for them. But when you take business from people who agree to sign paperwork just to give you their assets, you might be signing up for something you'll later regret.

In the video library, there is a video that compares our profession to that of a dentist. Many go to the dentist reluctantly, yet some think very highly of their dentists and want to refer them to others because of the great care and service they provide. Far too many savers are reluctant to go to a financial advisor because they fear being a victim of the old-school predator vs. prey model.

And you know what? It doesn't have to be that way!

Working with great people encourages working with more great people through great referrals.

If you're driven solely by revenue, you will work with people you probably shouldn't. When you agree to be someone's financial advisor, you are committing yourself to them and their families for the rest of their lives. Be careful about taking business from someone if you feel like you're doing them a favor but they don't appreciate it. If this is the situation, the odds are not in your favor that you will have a good relationship down the road. It's best to take business from people who are excited for you to be responsible to them and their financial future. If they don't seem to appreciate it, don't commit to the relationship. A great dentist has a thriving office full of referrals and happy clients who are making the very best of the necessary mouth maintenance. You can be the very best version of yourself and multiply your favorite clients by elevating their experience with you and your office.

I've been told many times, "Happy wife = happy life." And in our business, happy clients = happy life.

Once you commit to serving a client, in general, we at ShiftMethods feel it is not appropriate to "fire" him or her. Six years ago, a couple was referred to me, and the husband—a physician—was not exactly the epitome of kindness, but he did seem to value our service. As a result, I was concerned how it may go in the future. I knew he could benefit greatly from our process, yet I was not completely comfortable working with him. I did commit myself to him, and what I feared came upon me. Each interaction we had with him and his wife got harder and harder. And then his wife got Parkinson's disease. The reviews in our office became even more difficult. Then all of a sudden, things changed.

A couple of years ago, he came into my office. By that time, his wife was very sick. I noticed his attitude to be significantly more positive. After our review, he said, "You know, George, I have to apologize to you. You have been committed and kind to me and have taken care of me and my family, but I have not been kind to you. I want to tell you I'm sorry for that."

I said, "Well, Doctor, I appreciate your telling me that, but what's changed?"

He replied, "I realize how hard you've worked for me and how hard I've been on you. Yet you stuck with me. In the past when we met, I was stressed out with my medical practice, and recently I have been stressed out about my wife's illness. I took it out on you, and that's not fair to you. I want to tell you I am sorry."

That made me feel quite emotional. I knew I had been doing the right thing over the years, even though I was not getting appreciation from him. Seeing reconciliatory fruit from my labor is a driving force in serving. Giving always produces a multiplied effect.

If I felt like I could "fire" clients, I would have fired him. But I didn't because I had made a commitment to him and his wife. Fortunately, nearly all my clients are quite appreciative and a pleasure to serve. Keeping a close watch on the gate of who is coming in will help ensure that you have a gratifying book of business to serve.

If you notice during your initial interview that the potential client has a difficult personality, take note. I've had several people who initially struck me as "difficult people" later turn out to be great clients. We believe the reason lies in how they see us as professionals. What matters most is that savers see the value you can provide and that they see you as the "qualified professional" when it comes to managing their finances. If they don't value the effort from you or see you in that role, don't take them on as clients.

In the videos, we show you how to create an experience for them that exceeds their expectations and positions them to ask you (if applicable and appropriate), "Will you commit to taking responsibility for my family's finances?" And then you are the one who gets to decide, rather than being a victim of anyone who says yes.

Make a List Before You Start

When you're sitting with a client or getting near the close with a prospect, and they have questions or concerns, it is extremely important to get a list of all the concerns and questions that are on their minds before you start answering them. The more you know about what they would like to discuss, the better prepared you will be to make *their* most important thing *your* most important thing.

If you address issues only as they are brought up, it can feel like "dodging bullets." More importantly, you may never get to the most important underlying motivation of the issues, or you may get off track spending too much time talking about something that's not as important to them. Whether on the phone or in person, when savers have questions or concerns, get the entire list before you start to address any of them. When you do this, positive things happen:

1. It gives you context of what's on their mind.
2. They feel listened to.
3. It gives you time to formulate a response that addresses all their thoughts in an order that makes sense and they can understand.

Avoid the temptation to volley back and forth with questions and answers. This is not the most efficient or effective way.

We've had clients spend five to ten minutes explaining things they would like to hear about, talk about, or have more questions about. Something powerful happens when savers hear themselves say something and when they see that you are listening well to what's on their minds.

How Our Process Created Clarification for Gloria and Her Husband

Here's an example of how that plays out during a client interview. A husband and wife were referred to me and became my clients. I met with them three times but had not yet done paperwork to initiate the process of doing business together. During that time, they interviewed three other financial professionals. As I spoke with them, their recollection of some of the things we had talked about in our office was completely inaccurate. When I began the meeting, I started asking them, as I do in every meeting, "Last time we were together, you mentioned... (I summarized the list of things they had brought up in the past). Are there any other concerns you have in planning and preparing for retirement?"

The wife, whom we will call Gloria, began telling me some things she said I had told them before—things she did not like. These were not things I had told her. But rather than quickly defending myself, and attempting to correct her inaccuracies immediately, I wrote them down item by item, line by line. Gloria mentioned eleven things she recalled from our previous meetings that concerned her.

What made it very difficult for me is that seven of them were completely inaccurate. When she was done bringing up her list of concerns, I politely went through them item by item, in some cases reminding her of previous discussions we had had. I went through the same explanations I had gone through before. In doing that, Gloria and her husband recalled the talks we had before. As a result, they felt listened to, they felt relieved, and now they felt like they were understood. They felt like they understood the solution strategy I was presenting to them.

Had I not taken time to listen to them thoroughly, I may have felt defensive ("Ma'am, I already told you..."), they would have felt the need to be right, and we probably would not have done business together. This is a case in which I won out over the other advisors (as ShiftMethods advisors normally do). When asked afterward, they said the reason was because I was attentive, forthright, and made things easy for them to understand.

Shifting Your Methods

Do a quick self-assessment. On a scale of 1 (lowest) to 10 (highest), how skilled do you think you are at the following?

Important Skill	Your Self-Rating
a. Being a facilitator who allows both you and your clients to discover their needs	_____

b. Asking great questions to gather the most information possible to enable you to be of optimum benefit to savers _____

c. Asking "What else?" multiple times (See chapter 4.) _____

d. Offering your solution at the ideal moment and not rushing it _____

e. Tailoring your solutions based on the concerns each saver shares with you *and* the needs you see _____

f. Encouraging savers to continue doing what has gone well in their saving approach _____

g. Empathizing with savers in the challenges they've faced over the years by asking good questions and listening to understand what is important to them _____

h. Evaluating how your clients' current plans are aligned to give them the results they expect going forward _____

i. Avoiding feeling frustrated when a prospect just doesn't get it _____

CHAPTER 3
Nine Ways ShiftMethods Advisors Are Different

Learning ShiftMethods creates a shift in your mind-set. Many advisors have been exposed to traditional sales methods for so long that ShiftMethods revolutionizes every aspect of their interactions with savers. The result: it's hard to adjust.

Before we examine the traits that make ShiftMethods advisors different, let's look at the traditional sales method and how it often alienates our prospects and clients.

The Traditional Approach: "Predator vs. Prey"

Some people consider me to be the rebel in the financial services business because I am so vocal about what many are thinking yet few speak of. This business tends to be highly ego-based, and people don't appreciate my saying that in general, there is often a real disdain for clients. A lot of salespeople in all types of business, not just ours, dislike their clients because their clients are "high-maintenance" or because "they don't get it." Salespeople complain that their clients don't do what they recommend. But I believe the problem is not with the clients at all; the problem lies in our traditional selling approach and mind-set.

As mentioned earlier, I observe traditional sales as "predator vs. prey." Too often, financial advisors are taught to attempt to convince prospects that their own products are the best without taking time or interest to determine what is most important to the clients and what is *good* about their current plan.

Many of us have seen the nearly inhumane portrayal of the stock broker of hopeful investors in movies like *Boiler Room* and *Wolf of Wall Street*. Unfortunately, many firms would likely be embarrassed if some of their "sales tactics" that were taught in closed-door sessions were exposed.

This is not for you.

The highest form of salesmanship—the one we must strive for—is to be facilitators who seek to benefit savers rather than "peddling a product." This is how we can think differently.

Many of the commonly used methods of presentation and selling make things much more complex for the saver than they need to be, leaving them befuddled and less confident about their financial future.

And you know what? It doesn't have to be that way!

Let's Expose Our Tactics
It is important to create a solution strategy to position the savers retirement assets to get what they expect over a long-term. Our

THINK DIFFERENTLY

ShiftMethods-trained advisors' experience has been that nearly all of people's perceived fears and concerns can be heard with a proper process.

The traditional approach is for the financial advisor to drive the interaction with clients to convince, explain, and ultimately *sell* them a product. Savers sense this, and it is a turnoff to them, either consciously or subconsciously. With ShiftMethods, you are listening to clients describe their situations, challenges, and dreams and responding with encouragement, empathy, enlightenment to a better way, and finally, ultimately, with a solution strategy that will address everything they share with you in an optimum way.

In our experience, a tremendous opportunity exists to radically increase the success and satisfaction of you and your clients. You and your clients will experience the fact that there are much better ways to connect the saver's needs to the facilitator's expertise. With a good interaction, both parties always win. With a typical interaction, both parties remain unsure of the future. Unfortunately, many savers feel that salespeople try to force or coerce a fit.

And you know what? It doesn't have to be that way!

The word "selling" is tainted with the connotation of someone doing something to somebody. It often feels like someone needs to lose for the other to win. Neither party wants to feel that way. The salesperson doesn't want to feel like a predator, and the prospect doesn't want to feel like prey. Under the traditional sales model, even talented and caring sales professionals can be assumed guilty until proven innocent when accused. Unfortunately, the sales-process interaction often feels like "fear-based selling." Rare is the saver who has not felt somehow abused by a "sales professional" through perceived manipulation, dishonesty, or even incompetence. ShiftMethods puts you and your clients on the same side of the table, as equal partners in bringing their vision to life.

With ShiftMethods, everyone wins every time.

Also, dysfunctional *buying* practices have arisen to accommodate dysfunctional *selling* practices. We call this "commoditization." You and I both know that it's difficult to oversimplify the products we represent; they are complex. If savers cannot differentiate you as a caring professional whose biggest priority is being of benefit to them, if there is a reason to do "financial business," you are just like everyone else…a suit peddling a product. Both parties hate having their time wasted, but that is exactly what happens with dysfunctional selling practices.

Now let's look at the behaviors and characteristics that make ShiftMethods advisors unique and highly successful.

1. ShiftMethods Advisors Are Great Listeners

Often, the more you talk, the less people are interested in hearing what you have to say. Conversely, the more you listen well and minimize talk, asking great questions and, when appropriate, telling thought-provoking stories, the more interested clients are in hearing what you have to say.

Imagine going into the doctor's office, and the doctor asks you how you are feeling. As soon as you start to describe your ailment, she interrupts and starts pontificating about the latest and greatest wonder drug that is extremely popular with her patients. You sit there in disbelief, wondering what is happening and wondering if a candid camera is hidden somewhere, and someone is going to pop out and say it's all a joke. That never happens at the doctor's office, right? Instead, the doctor asks many relevant questions, performs a few tests, asks a few more questions, and then starts talking about possible strategies to resolve your condition. In fact, in my experience, by the time a doctor with great bedside manner is ready to recommend treatment, I have long since been ready to take action.

This is how it works with ShiftMethods facilitators. We've invested appropriately in understanding and analysis. When it is time to recommend the solution strategy, the client has been ready for a while. In fact, with a properly conducted process, clients feel like they are waiting for you to describe the solution strategy and how to implement it. They are waiting for you to say you will commit yourself and your resources to them and their families for the rest of their lives.

2. They Are Skilled at Going Beyond Theme-Based Selling

Several financial professionals have developed niche markets from "shared client interests." This may be fine for some, but it can create unnecessary tension.

Using ShiftMethods, we work with advisors to create a deep understanding of their clients without muddying the waters with social awkwardness. Many advisors have clients who are drawn to them because they are avid hunters or sports fanatics or have some other binding form of connection. This often works well, to some extent.

In some cases, however, advisors who build a niche of clients who are similar to themselves discover that the professional relationship can be secondary to the social relationship. This can lead to difficulty because the boundaries of the relationship can come into question. In the long term, mutual resentment can develop with certain individuals because they feel a social obligation that puts pressure on the professional relationship. The concern here is burnout—feeling too much emotional energy being drawn from certain people.

The primary draw for any new referral should always be your stand-alone, superior abilities as a financial professional. We will always have great clients who are also close friends; however, we find that having intentional boundaries with our clients creates better *professional* and *social* relationships—and more of them.

ShiftMethods teaches financial sales professionals to be facilitators by seeking first to understand. A natural by-product of seeking to understand is creating a relationship in which the client values your insight. It just makes sense. If savers feel like they are understood by a professional they respect, the natural progression is to defer to the professional who knows them and is capable. The governing philosophy of ShiftMethods is to create an environment in which the financial professional understands the saver and the saver views the financial professional as capable of facilitating clients getting what they expect and, most importantly, avoiding regret.

"Mutual exploration" refers to the facilitator exploring what savers' needs are and the savers exploring what their needs are as well. Imagine inviting savers on a journey of exploration of their own mind-sets, tendencies, and preferences. This is important because often, savers do not take a very close look at what they have, why they have what they have, how it may or may not benefit them, and what their alternatives are. Your major role is to facilitate that exploration. If you determine that something is missing, then help them discover what it is and what the solution can be.

3. They Strive to Be the Best Version of Themselves

How do you really see yourself, your service, and the impact you make on your clients? Be honest with yourself. Your answer will not be graded as good or bad, but is merely a gut check of how you really see your role.

With ShiftMethods, we see that what we do is the difference between life and death, financially. If you are not completely convinced that what you do is the literal difference between financial life and death, you are either in the wrong business or you need some facilitation of enlightenment to discover the magnitude of impact you make. If you honestly don't see yourself as excelling in this area, relax—ShiftMethods will uncover your passion and help you be the best version of yourself.

If there is a way to summarize ShiftMethods teaching, it is *listening to clients well, and helping you become the best version of yourself to serve them well.* Let's face it, there is an unlimited supply of marketing techniques and client sales strategies. We've done exhaustive research on how advisors sell and how clients buy. We have found that, although there are some similarities in some subgroups, everyone is different enough that there is no "one size fits all" approach for selling or buying. But there *is* a "one size fits all" approach for facilitating because a key component of ShiftMethods is *relationship.*

For a relationship to thrive, there must be *understanding*. To have understanding, there must be *listening*. To be an efficient listener, you must ask *great questions*, for prospects' sake. In all the research we have done, we have yet to meet someone who does not desire to be understood. This is a common thread among humans, no matter who they are. When you understand, you are in a position to serve. When you serve, you thrive, and your clients are happy and want to tell everyone they know all about their experience.

You provide value to everyone you meet by gathering information, establishing trust, discovering where you may be able to provide value, and giving that value freely. It's a perpetual and cumulative experience—the more genuine interest you demonstrate, the more information you gather, the more trust is felt, and the more likely you're able to provide value—and the more likely you are to be referred.

4. They Have Intangible Measures of Ability

Here are three characteristics that can lead to success. ShiftMethods advisors exhibit these winning traits:

- **Intelligence quotient, or IQ**—Years ago, this measure was used to separate the intellectually capable from the deficient. Although the ability to learn is very important, today, many examples show that belief system and determination are much more consistent markers to predict success.
- **Emotional quotient**—EQ is the ability to listen and understand, know, or empathize with how another person is feeling. It's the ability to know how much you should be pressing for information and how good of a connection

you have with a client. I like to refer to this as the primary tool needed to build "relational equity."

- **Execution quotient**—This is the ability to follow a process consistently while adapting and adjusting appropriately based on each unique situation. And, maybe more important for high achievement, it's the ability to be self-aware and build feedback loops into the process to know if you're on the best track or if you are missing something.

You can develop and improve all these characteristics further. Blending these three characteristics can enable an amateur salesperson to experience big, consistent success versus intermediate pockets of moderate success. And it can lead a great professional salesperson to find extreme success consistently.

5. Their Strategies Are Flexible

Let's face it, things change, and when they do, your strategy must be capable of being modified.

Clients' situations change, the economy changes, and financial tools change. But one thing that will likely never change is the facilitator who endeavors to serve clients and their families in getting what they expect and avoiding regret. We encourage facilitators to be candid with their clients in highlighting the importance of *a proper solution strategy and flexibility* to adapt and adjust with changing situations, markets, and tools available. Do you see the power of the last statement? "Proper solution strategy and flexibility."

The proper strategy includes a collection of appropriate financial tools that has the highest probability that clients will look back on their choices and be pleased, and the lowest probability that they will look back on their choices with regret.

A proper strategy with flexibility creates value to the saver. This is the service we provide in exchange for payment. Fortunately, in this great financial business, we are capable of being compensated at levels far beyond what many could have ever imagined. It is a great responsibility to shepherd large amounts of retirement assets that people have saved and that have grown over many years. Being a facilitator to protect, preserve, and grow wealth in the most effective and efficient way deserves great reward. We believe you should never be bashful about being well compensated.

Your work is worth significantly more to others than you could even imagine. As you become the best version of yourself, it only stands to reason, you will be much better compensated. Based on our experience in working with both new and seasoned advisors, when you begin introducing ShiftMethods concepts into your practice, you will look back on the new beginning as a turning point in development of your craft.

We believe every decision in life is a risk/reward play. For example, every time we cross an intersection, we risk getting hit by a vehicle. Some might say it's a low risk, while others might consider it a high risk. And investing in a high-probability startup company may seem almost like a guarantee...a sure thing, a no-brainer, a low risk. But we may call it high risk. You get the picture. In a nutshell, when you are a proper facilitator, your clients will have a strategy they are comfortable with that will position them to get the results (reward) they expect, and most importantly, ensure the highest probability of avoiding regret (risk of disappointment).

6. They Understand the Saver's Train Wreck—Loss Aversion

We talk a lot about avoiding regret because studies show that humans have a 2:1 emotion-to-loss aversion. Because of human nature, we fear loss at twice the extent that we seek gain. For example, I'm not going to bet on something unless I feel like I have at least 2-to-1 odds to win. This means that a client avoiding a 10 percent loss is equivalent to the client seeking a 20 percent gain. Because of our human nature, we will keep what we have rather than risk loss in the order of magnitude of 2 to 1.

Now, the way the stock market behaves, the magnitude of loss to gain is 1 to 2.5 (1:2.5). That's what often makes people feel super uncomfortable. History shows that if my portfolio got a 10 percent rate of return over the past thirty years, I would have had to tolerate an approximate 25 percent downward fluctuation at multiple times in the process of getting that 10 percent return, on average.

Because of our human-nature loss-aversion tendencies, we subconsciously think, "I want to get a 10 percent return, but I don't want to have to go down any more than 5 percent in the process." So, when the market takes a downward turn of 15 or 20 percent, people get nervous. They get uncomfortable. They start thinking they need to change their path and do something different instead of letting it work itself out. That's the tendency.

The problem with that strategy going forward into the future from today is although the past thirty years have yielded well through the sometimes-drastic bumps, you don't know if you're going to average a 10 percent return going forward, even if you *are* willing to tolerate the downward fluctuation of 25 percent.

You don't know what's going to happen in the future. You know that historically, your portfolio could earn 10 percent, even though the market went down 25 percent multiple times in the process.

But projecting into the future, saying that you're willing to tolerate a 25 percent downturn doesn't mean you're going to get a 10 percent rate of return over time. Often, we talk with clients who say, "Well, I have broad shoulders. I can handle this and tolerate it." But that doesn't mean they're going to when in the middle of the circumstances. Boxing legend Mike Tyson made the comment, "Everyone has a plan until they get punched in the face." There are no guarantees in the stock market. When you get "punched in the face" with an unexpected event, your resulting reaction can range from feeling paralyzed to making erratic decisions. Neither is good. Knowing your clients, their tendencies, and their likely reactions in dire moments will help you position their assets for sustainability, to avoid regret.

Too often, people make abrupt changes in their saving strategy because they can't stand what they are experiencing and are unable to stick to the plan. In many cases, a big problem with a plan is not sticking to it. If you stuck to a plan that wasn't even a great plan, you would do better than changing a great plan midstream. Ideally, you have a plan you are comfortable with, in terms of performance and the range of value you're going to experience, and it meets your objectives. Where people get themselves in trouble is having short-term memories. Our aversion to loss, or our loss-avoidance disposition, causes us to feel like we must do something when we see that we are losing. And that's a disaster. It's a train wreck that should be avoided.

The best plan is the one that's best for the client. It meets the client's performance numbers. He or she is comfortable in the process and able to keep the train on the track (adhering to the solutions strategy), regardless of market conditions.

I believe this is why so many financial brokers and clients are frustrated. The markets give you what they give you, and all you can do is attempt to make some adjustments and hope it gets better in the future. This emotional roller coaster of good times and bad creates great stress.

But you know what? It doesn't have to be that way!

Using ShiftMethods, it is possible to know enough about your clients to facilitate them getting what they expect going forward as they plan for retirement.

7. They Agree with Prospects Who Are "All Set"

"All set" is a reflex response people often say when they don't feel they need anyone's help. For example, someone walks into a department store, and a salesperson asks if she can help. The customer says, "No, I'm all set. I'm just looking." Just looking for what? Dust on the floor? A burned-out lightbulb? If you are in a department store, you likely cannot help thinking about what's on display, or something may catch your eye. The response of "All set" often has little to do with what's really happening. When you are meeting with prospects who say they are "all set," at the very minimum, they are curious. In addition, as we talk about in chapter 8, they may have FOMO (fear of missing out).

With ShiftMethods, when clients tell us they are "All set," we seek to prove their presumption that they are, in fact, "all set."

Right now, you may be cocking your head to the side like a dog that just heard a strange noise and is trying to figure it out. That's right—we seek to prove what our prospects hope to be true: "I'm all set." Just go with the flow. After all, who doesn't wish they were "all set" financially?

When you truly and wholeheartedly seek to do this, clients see it, feel it, and sincerely appreciate it. In our experience, if they are missing something significant, we nearly always gain a client. Conversely, if they are, in fact, all set, we often get multiple referrals.

We had an advisor who had begun to sprinkle ShiftMethods practices into his client interviews and saw an increase of revenue of more than $100,000 in the first five months of subscription. He credits much of his quick jump in revenue to going with the flow with prospects.

He said, "If they say they are all set, who am I to disagree with their perspective?" After using ShiftMethods, he said, "This stuff just makes sense. I have been taught for twenty-one years to find or create pain, convince, sell, and always be closing, but with ShiftMethods, prospects become clients just because I am asking great questions, listening, understanding them, serving them, and giving them feedback about how their assets are aligned with what is most important to them. It is much easier than I thought."

8. They Delay Gratification and Offer the Solution at the Ideal Time

Top sales professionals avoid premature solutions. They can continue to drill down and discover exactly what the saver needs and what his or her concerns are. When the interview is done well, the facilitator not only discovers a deep understanding of the saver's situation, but the saver has a better understanding of his or her own situation.

Waiting for the ideal moment to offer the solution is a form of delayed gratification. When you see the potential for a solution, it's hard to keep from diving right in and presenting it. The hard part is to continue to accumulate information. It is hard because traditionally, sales professionals are taught to always be closing. They are taught that, when they see buying signals, "Go in for the kill." Thinking about that approach makes my belly hurt. It might be a decent strategy for some, but it is nowhere near the pinnacle of possibility for an expert salesperson.

It's so tempting to start moving toward a solution when you hear a problem the client mentions. But you must accumulate three to five strong reasons why you should be doing business with that prospect before you ever move into creating a solution. By the time you're ready to present a solution, the client will be asking these questions:

- "What can we do?"
- "How can we fix this?"
- "What are my options?"
- "How can you help me?"
- "Will you help us?"

This is important because we will miss the mark if we reveal a solution before we are certain about the complete list of concerns or challenges the savers face. They may get bored, their eyes will start to glaze over, and they will be not completely interested in what we are talking about. When we listen to their own story, their history, their background, and what brought them into the office, we can't help but understand. We must know well their basic motivation to be talking about their financial past, present and future with us. We need to accumulate all the ammunition we can to serve savers in a way that truly benefits them and exceeds their expectations.

9. They Know That When Savers Succeed, We All Win

Our intent when using ShiftMethods is to leave every interaction better than we found it and for our clients to have an experience meeting and working with us that exceeds their expectations so much so that they will reflect back on our time together and say, "Wow, I've never met anyone like her/him. I am so thankful for being introduced."

You are more successful when you can focus on the success of others rather than your own. This may sound like a tall order, but when you tell a new prospect your intent, not only do you affirm your own objective, you also recruit a team member. Prospects become mindful of your intent and look for clues that you are on track to accomplish your objective: serving them.

In a nutshell, when you tell savers that your bias is that you want them to have an experience that exceeds their expectations so much that they will say, "Wow, I've never met anyone like her/him," it communicates to them that they are getting ready for an "unfair exchange." You are giving them something exceptional. Whether you give them enlightenment to discover something about themselves or unprecedented feedback on how their assets align with their ultimate goals, they are, in fact, "all set." And you are the facilitator who traveled with them on their journey to financial fulfillment and the avoidance of regret.

Shifting Your Methods

1. We all want to be better. To what extent are you the best version of yourself?
2. Is there room for you to be more empathetic with savers, especially those it's hard for you to relate to because their situations are vastly different from your own?
3. Think about your typical client interview. What percentage of the time do you spend talking, and what percentage of the time do you spend listening? Commit to listening more of the time.
4. Assess the flexibility of your solutions. To what extent do you offer a proper strategy and flexibility to adapt and adjust with changing situations, markets, and tools available? What can you do to build more flexibility into your solutions?
5. If savers tell you they're "all set," do you tend to try to prove them wrong, or do you seek to prove them right? Make it your goal to prove them right, and let the discrepancies be uncovered naturally as the interview proceeds.

Bonus

Remember in the introduction, we talked about keeping the 90 percent of your process that is working well? If you are like many others, you will see that you are much better than what you may think.

Most training encourages you to jump ship from who you are and attempt to embrace a completely different way of doing things. We have seen from experience that this is often the wrong approach. We believe there is great value in facilitating your own discovery of what makes you who you are. All your future progress begins with building on the strengths you have. You are closer than what you think. Get free insights to help define the 90 percent that makes you do well, and highlight the 10 percent that, if adjusted over time, can multiply your effectiveness.

Go to www.shiftmethods.com/my90and10 to get your free insights.

CHAPTER 4
What Do Savers Really Want?

Not taking anything for granted is one of our biggest keys to success. The saver's story is vitally important to the big picture. Everyone attaches different meanings to the same words. Here's an example.

A woman says to her lawyer, "I want to divorce my husband."

He replies, "OK, on what grounds?"

She says, looking perplexed, "Grounds? Uh, well, we have two acres at the edge of town with a big lawn and some fruit trees."

"No, that's not what I meant," the lawyer says, a bit frustrated. "Ma'am, do you have a grudge?"

"Oh...yes, we have a two-car garage but only one car, so we use the rest for storage."

Getting exasperated, the lawyer asks, "Does he beat you up?"

"No," the wife replies. "I'm up by six-thirty, and sometimes he doesn't even get up until after I've left for work."

The attorney says curtly, *"Wait a minute. I'm trying to ask you WHY you want a divorce!"*

"We just can't seem to communicate."

• • •

This joke may sound funny, but it is certainly not funny to lose a relationship over poor communication. Words we use, the meanings they have for us and the savers—what we hear, what they hear—is all vitally important to great mutual understanding.

To ensure that we're truly communicating, we need to find out what savers are really saying. Everyone's meaning of certain terms or concepts is colored by their own personal background and experiences. We call this "connotation prejudice."

For example, we can ask what the connotation of the term "stock market" means to savers. That will bring us clarity about how they see the stock market. Here are some responses clients have given when we asked them what the term "stock market" means to them:

- "It's the only gig in town."
- "It's a necessary evil."
- "It's where you make money."
- "It's filled with crooks."

- "You lose money."
- "It works well over time."
- "It's about buying companies."
- "I hate the stock market."
- "I'm fascinated by it."

These different responses tell a little bit more about the saver and give you a better understanding of what his or her perspective is about the stock market. Being in the financial services business, we obviously have a completely different understanding from the general public about the meaning of the term "stock market."

Another word we ask savers about, in an effort to understand connotation prejudice, is "annuity." By simply asking what a saver's connotation is of the word "annuity," you can get a better understanding of his or her connotation prejudice. This enables you to determine if the savers have had a negative experience with annuities, if they're neutral toward them, or if they have had a positive experience with them. Simply asking the question does not insinuate that you're going to use that tool or that you're going to remove it from the saver's portfolio. You are simply asking what it means to him or her.

Watch for Incongruence

"Incongruence" is the difference between what you hear, what you expected to hear based on the accumulated conversation, and/or how a client's nonverbal cues are matching or not matching with the conversation. Observing what is happening in the interaction gives you great clues about what is happening internally with the saver. Good listeners pick up on these cues and find a way to discover what is behind the incongruence. Listen to what *is not* being said as you listen to what *is* being said. As Ralph Waldo Emerson said, "Your actions are so loud, I cannot hear what you are saying."

Watch the saver's actions, and look for incongruence and/or alignment with previous statements and the general theme of the interview.

Get Personal

During the interview, we encourage you to initiate "sidebar" conversations—conversations that may appear to be unrelated to the saver's finances. This is something that, as humans, we all tend to do. It is how we find common ground and relate to others. When you have a personal conversation with a saver, it automatically increases the relational equity. It allows you to build a relationship. As a result, the saver feels more comfortable sharing important personal information about his or her finances. Warning: we are not using this information against our prospects or clients! We are using it to benefit them. We know them, we care about them, we serve them, it exceeds their expectations, they appreciate it, they get the benefit of our elite service, we get another happy client, and of course, we get referrals.

For example, a client tells you he is very conservative financially, and then through personal conversation, you find out that on weekends, that client does motocross racing. That is valuable information. In general, a person who risks life and limb while racing is not conservative by nature. Exploring this type of discrepancy will bring clarity about who people really are, what motivates them, what they expect, and how you may aid in their avoiding regret.

When listening to savers, you get to know them. The better you know them, the better you serve them. For example, when you are made aware that someone is in a challenging situation, you can hardly help yourself from feeling empathy for that person and feeling like you want to do something to be of benefit to him or her. When you know people are in a challenging situation, it's easy to care for them and to want to help them. Knowing about a situation that's occurring in the saver's life creates caring and an ability to want to serve that person to alleviate his or her challenges.

Stay on Track

"Everyone has a plan until they get punched in the face." The saver interview can easily get way off track. What do you do when the saver starts asking you questions (sometimes hard questions that throw you off guard) while you are trying to go through your careful process to gather information?

This is extremely important. While you are attempting to gather more information about the saver, he or she will ask you specific questions. It is important to acknowledge them and to stay on task in gathering information. When a saver does this, it is important to continue to direct the conversation to avoid a premature solution presentation. It is a protection against unveiling an assumption you cannot help from making, even with the little interaction you had with the saver.

It's easy to start thinking, "I know where this is going…I've seen it before." But you must let the interview play out naturally and not hit the fast-forward button in your mind.

This is a critical time. We need to stay focused on gathering information so that, at the appointed time, we are well equipped to give them the complete feedback and answers they are seeking. The way we do this is by softening and directing the conversation. Let's say a saver asks you, "Is this something you could help me with?" Rather than saying "Yes, I can fix that, and here's how...," it's better to say something like, "We have many clients who have similar versions of what you just described, but what we find is that everyone's situation is unique. Can you tell me a little bit more about it?"

Or, when the client asks the question, respond, "I could talk about that topic for hours! Can you be a little bit more specific about exactly what you would like to know about?" Be sure to give them some form of answer. There are many examples of these in video format in the ShiftMethods library that describe specific scenarios and explain exactly what to say when someone asks questions that throw off your process. Knowing how to respond can prevent you from losing control of the interview and missing out on benefiting the saver because you are not prepared to respond to questions outside your process.

For now, write down the specific questions clients frequently ask so you can be sure to come back and give them complete answers as they apply in their particular case. Make sure they know you have taken note and will be sure to come back to the topic and give them a complete answer. And make sure you follow up and do it!

Assignment: Create a solution response for any situation that happens more than a few times. This will prevent interviews from getting off track. If you are getting off track, losing a sale, or not closing as many as you prefer, guess what? It doesn't have to be that way!

Experience Can Make Us Deaf

Previous advisor experience and assumptions can be one of the most dangerous obstacles in attempting to serve savers.

The more savers you serve, the more stories you hear about financial challenges, and the more likely it is that you will make assumptions about what the typical person wants or needs. Because you have seen so many new people over the years, it is easy to be tempted to "know where this is going." This is very dangerous! If we're thinking, "I've heard this a thousand times," then we aren't listening to the saver's concerns. We are tuning out these very important people. We become deaf to their concerns. That is not helpful to anyone.

Remember, when you are interviewing a new saver, this may be a similar version of a story you've heard hundreds of times, but it's the first time for this client, so listen with big ears.

Savers will tell you exactly how it is for them. It may sound quite similar to other stories you've heard, but their version is different—it's unique to them. Don't guess. Don't assume! Don't turn a deaf ear to their very real concerns. Listen, listen, listen, listen, listen. Have big ears.

The Most Important Interview Question of All: "What Else?"

We read in many psychology books that it's wise to seek first to understand and then to be understood. This is a critical part of the ShiftMethods philosophy. It means investing what seems like large amounts of time, which is actually a matter of minutes, to understand savers and exactly what they are hoping to accomplish.

With ShiftMethods, the question we encourage you to ask savers is *not* "What keeps you up at night?" or "Where do you think the problem lies?" or "What brings you in here today?" Instead, the question we ask is very simply, "What are your biggest concerns as you plan and prepare for retirement?"

Listen to their responses. Now, what comes next is *the most important part of the book!* If you get nothing else from this book, please understand this. When people mention their concerns, do this:

> Listen intently, write notes so you don't forget, and then reply, "What else?"
> And then,
> Listen intently, write notes so you don't forget, and then reply, "What else?"
> And then,
> Listen intently, write notes so you don't forget, and then reply, "What else?"
> And then,
> Listen intently, write notes so you don't forget, and then reply, "What else?"
> And then,
> Keep attentively asking "What else?" until they say, "That is all. There is nothing else."

Ask "What else?" as many times as necessary to get all their thoughts and concerns on the table. Mysteriously, you and the saver will discover hidden motivations, preferences, and tendencies during this exchange.

Be prepared to pause when necessary throughout this exchange. It may take fifteen to twenty minutes to have savers go through their own discovery of their biggest concerns about planning and preparing for retirement at this stage. We say "at this stage" because as life goes on, our perspective changes. Concerns that savers never had in the past begin to appear as they go through different stages. Conversely, concerns they may have had for years may have gone away.

The questions you are asking now may be questions they've asked themselves a similar version of before, but it may have been a long time ago. And now, when you ask them the question as they are sitting there with you, the facilitator, somehow the answer becomes more real and more in-depth; it creates mutual understanding and a relational connection.

Often, when I meet with someone new in the office and ask them what their biggest concerns are, they will start with something like long-term care or wanting to make sure they have enough money or thinking their investments could do better. These are all common phrases, and it's important to know exactly what these topics mean to each individual saver.

For example, suppose you ask a saver, "What about long-term care concerns you?" She will tell you exactly what she thinks (maybe a story of her aunt who is in a nursing home and is having a terrible experience) and why she brought up the topic. But don't just take that at face value. When she finishes her explanation, say, "What else?"

When a saver says, "We want to make sure we have enough money," don't just take that at face value. Ask him, "What about making sure you have enough money concerns you?" Or "What is your concern about not having enough money?" Or "If you didn't feel like you had enough, what would that mean?" When you ask these questions, it automatically facilitates the saver explaining to you the *why* behind the *what*. It's most important to ask, "What else?" after they tell you every *why*.

If the saver says, "We think our investments could do better," say, "Tell me more about your investments doing better." After he speaks, then, of course, follow up with the question "What else?" Now is not the time to agree, disagree, or solve. Just keep listening and drawing out the *why* behind the *what.*

After every new question, keep asking "What else?" When you do this, you will get to the bottom of the motivation, need, hurt, or historical event that is the root of their initial response. As a good listener, you are more interested in the *why* than the *what.* Keep asking "What else?" until they say, "That's all. There is nothing else." This is what truly reveals the critical information for you and the prospect. In the second or third "What else?" is often where the most important information lies.

There are two main reasons for this exercise:

1. The saver feels like you are listening to him or her (because you are).
2. It allows you to get a much better understanding of exactly how savers think and what they want.

Pain, Gain, and Novelty

Savers are, in essence, moving toward or away from various sensations:

Pain: "This is going badly, and I need to change."
Gain: "I want greater return on my investment relative to my exposure."
Novelty: "I want parts of my plan to be unique and interesting—something exciting to talk about."

Human beings, regardless of what they would like to think about themselves, are naturally trained to respond to pain, gain, and/or novelty. As you conduct the interview, it will be obvious to you which motivates the saver. In the ShiftMethods material, we discuss specifics of what to look for to understand what is motivating the saver you are meeting with.

People who are trying to move *away from pain* will often tell you about things in their strategy that are painful for them:

- "I don't want to lose."
- "I'm afraid that something bad is going to happen."
- "I'm paying too much in fees for what I'm getting."

People who are trying to move *toward gain* will say things like this:

- "I need to get more for the time my investments have been growing."
- "I think we can do better."
- "I'm not sure I'm going to have enough if I don't start earning more."

They will talk about goals, objectives, and desires they have for something more.

People who are trying to move *toward novelty* want to have it all. They want to be able to have their investments do what they expect, be protected if something goes wrong, and leave as much as possible to their heirs. And they are often vocal about their excitement about having a uniquely strategic plan. Often, novelty is the sweet spot.

Stories Relate and Facilitate Understanding

We use stories to enlighten and understand. I read a book long ago that encouraged "story selling." In concept, I agree. However, the author missed the greatest benefit of stories—we use stories to relate to and understand our clients. We use stories about situations in which others have made choices that may be similar to what the saver we are sitting with may tend to benefit from. We don't tell people what to do. We don't try to convince. We tell stories of others in similar situations simply to encourage the prospects we are sitting with to consider the possibility and to get their thoughts on how they relate to the story.

This is a non-confrontational method of introducing a concept or new idea. After all, we are not asking our prospects to do what the one in the story did, yet they cannot help but relate with the story on some level (even if it is in disagreement).

The most important part of the story is what happens next. When you finish a story, the saver will make a comment like, "That sounds a lot like me except…" or "I'm nothing like that because I'd rather…" or "That sounds just like me." This is the most important part of the story because this is when you get a better understanding of how they think, what their biases are, and what their preconceived and maybe inaccurate notions are.

With the ShiftMethods process, we use stories to relate, to introduce concepts, and most importantly, to gain a better understanding of the people we are sitting with. As they share their own stories, they cannot help but feel more comfortable and confident in you as a professional in your ability to care for them when you listen and understand their own perspective. People who listen are people who care.

Pay Attention to the Yellow Lights

When driving a vehicle, it has become universally acceptable to speed through a yellow light instead of stopping. In business, when you sense a yellow light, you need to slow down—in fact, it is imperative that you slow down. It is often much easier to just gloss over a topic, or fast-forward to avoid the uncomfortable feeling of asking a question that should be asked.

Here are some questions to ask yourself to determine if you might be rushing some important elements of your client interviews:

- What assumptions am I making about my prospects?
- What questions could I be asking that I am not asking?
- Why am I not asking the questions I could be asking?
- Do I feel uncomfortable? Why?
- Am I concerned about how the saver might respond? Why?
- Do I think I know the answer to the question—have I made an assumption?
- What else?

You might not remember that you ran all those yellow lights until the prospect says, "That's interesting. You've given me a lot to think about" and then disappears.

But that is what often happens. You sense or hear a "yellow light" comment and just keep on moving, hoping your charm and intelligence will overcome them and they will concede to being your client. Fortunately, that is rarely the case. The ShiftMethods process encourages seeking a solid foundation on which to build a strong, deep, mutual understanding.

We've all developed an acute ability to sense yellow lights. However, we can make a habit of overlooking or ignoring those yellow lights because they can be uncomfortable and require us to slow down. When we sense a yellow light, we must slow down. If we don't slow down, it may penalize us heavily in the long run. Don't let the failure to yield at a yellow light steal your privilege to serve.

Not every person we meet is going to be our client. Sometimes we are going to come across legitimate red lights. There can be legitimate reasons for us to not do business with a prospect. If someone truly is "all set" or is not qualified, *we have no business attempting to create something from nothing.*

In the past, we may have been introduced to prospects whom we did not end up doing business with because of missed yellow lights. As you go through the ShiftMethods material and commit yourself to being more sensitive to and aware of what's happening in your interactions with the savers you are introduced to, you will become a hound dog for yellow lights. You will sniff them out, hone in on them, and most importantly, (through the videos), find a way to ask the right questions to determine what's behind them.

Yellow lights can be doubts, fears, concerns, challenges, and hard questions. Yellow lights can also be a change in behavior, seat position, eye contact, tone of voice, or the level of engagement. In the ShiftMethods library, you will learn to use all these indicators to anticipate if a yellow light is present.

You may have a solution that clearly benefits the client and puts her in a better position, yet she doesn't buy it. Why? Often, it's because a yellow light has been glossed over, or several yellow lights, and the prospect subconsciously does not feel comfortable moving forward. If you ask the client why, she probably will not be able to articulate exactly why. She just knows that she doesn't quite feel comfortable. She will tell you something like, "That's interesting. I need some time to think about it." When this happens, you both lose! You lose the opportunity to serve the saver, and she loses the privilege of having you be her trusted professional.

Here are some things you can say to uncover what's behind a yellow light. Pause in the conversation and, without sounding accusing, say something like this:

- "I have a concern…"
- "I am confused…"
- "I think we may have a problem."

When you say this, it stops the conversation and sheds necessary light on what just happened. Politely recognize what you just observed that caused you to stop the conversation.

Be Curious

Note: You are not calling savers out or exposing them. You're simply noting a change and being curious to gain a better understanding. Ask a polite yet direct question to help understand what's behind what you observed. This is difficult to convey and explain in writing. That's why we use videos—so you can get a clearer understanding of these behaviors, changes, and interactions.

These are high-level interaction skills. Remember, the reason we're working so hard to understand what savers need is *to serve them well!* Good questions demonstrate our knowledge and expertise. After all, to ask good questions, you must have a good understanding, a good knowledge base, and experience to know where to focus with the saver.

Good listening is the single most important key to your success. What are you listening to? Asking great questions is like fitting together many complex parts to a machine of understanding, mutual respect, and relational equity so you can provide great service to the saver. By politely and carefully asking great questions, you will hear prospects say things that they have never heard themselves say. You will draw them out and facilitate mutual discovery of what is most important to them, and most importantly, the *why* behind the *what*.

Use the client's words as much as possible. If the client uses metaphors, use those metaphors when it's your turn to talk. In ShiftMethods training, you will see how to use metaphors relative to a saver's vocation, where he lives, his interests, and other areas. We work hard to be relatable, and using metaphors helps facilitate mutual understanding.

Effective communication is critical in building relationships. Having big ears will enhance your interactions with your prospects and clients and enable you to be of more benefit to them. And that benefits everyone.

Shifting Your Methods

1. How skilled are you at picking up on "incongruence," or a gap between what savers are saying and what their non-verbal body language is suggesting? If you haven't been

in tune with your clients' body language, pay closer attention to it to find out if they are saying something they don't mean, for whatever reason.
2. How comfortable are you about talking with your prospects and clients about their personal lives? Do you tend to stick to business? Try being more intentional about "sidebar" conversations. This will facilitate relationship building and identify interests your clients might have in common with you or someone you know.
3. Write down three to five comments or questions your prospects make that can be a "punch in the face" and lure you into presenting a premature solution. The longer you are in the business, the more consistency you will see with this. Then write down a response you can make to soften and direct, to continue to gather more information before presenting a premature solution.
4. Practice asking, "What else?" in all your communications, with your clients and with your family members, friends, and colleagues. When someone reveals something important, we often respond immediately, taking it only at face value. Practice asking, "What else?" until there *is* nothing else.
5. How good are you at pausing at the "yellow lights" in your conversations with clients? When you sense a discrepancy or concern, how likely are you to stop and ask for clarification? Do you tend to fast-forward because the "yellow light" is uncomfortable? Those caution signals are important. Work on acknowledging them and asking questions to get to the heart of the matter.
6. What are some "yellow lights" you have sped through in the past? How could you have slowed down in those specific situations?

7. To what extent do you use stories to illustrate thoughts and the impact of potential solutions? People love stories, and their responses to your stories will offer you a lot of insight about their biases and situations. Think about listening to their comments after the story to learn more about their disposition.

Bonus

"Yellow lights" are deal killers. For more yellow lights and how to avoid them, go to www.shiftmethods.com/yellowlights.

CHAPTER 5
Our Role: To Listen and Understand

In today's information age, we have more information than we could ever use available to us instantly on the Internet. If you have a problem or need information, you can type it into Google and find a plethora of tools, resources, and potential solutions. The financial services business boasts an ever-increasing array of financial products that are inundating the marketplace. But a significant gap is forming. Something extremely important is missing: the ability of the saver to be listened to, heard, and understood so that he or she can find the best collection of products and tools to fit his or her disposition. What's often missing is *empathic connection.*

Savers' subconscious hope is that someone will ask them what they're looking for, help them discover what they have (how close they are to being on track and "all set"), see how what they have is aligned with what is most important to them, and, if needed, get what they have properly aligned. Explain how the solution strategy works, take them through the entire process of implementation, and finally, carefully monitor it to make appropriate adjustments along the way as needed. Today's sales professionals are great at telling you the features and the benefits of products, but most rare is the professional who does a complete job of listening to people, finding out exactly what they want, and sticking with savers so they can retire happily ever after.

A Great Consequence of Listening

When you listen to people, you can't help but develop an affection for them because you're hearing their life stories. And then they will know that you care about them. They will listen to you because you've listened to them. It sounds basic and simple, but most people just don't listen well. They say they do; they talk about being a "trusted advisor," and they use industry buzzwords. But really, they're often just pitching products.

When you're pitching a great product, you will close well. And when you really *listen* to people and truly understand their needs and goals, you will close extremely well and ensure the solution strategy you implement is the very best for the saver and their unique situation. This is because everyone who talks with you sees how you, your character, and your process are different than what they've experienced in the past.

What People Want

What do savers want?

I've asked this question in many seminars for financial advisors. Without exception, I get confident, affirming, enthusiastic responses like these:

- "They want to protect their money."
- "They want to grow their money."

- "They want to know that they can produce income."
- "They want peace of mind."
- "They want to reduce their taxes."

The list goes on, but the real answer to the question is "I don't know. I'd have to ask them first."

Let's not guess about what savers want, what brought them to the office, or their financial upbringing. Let's ask them!

This is tough. We've been there, we've done it, we've seen almost all of it—many times over. There is so much repetition for us as advisors. But we must remember that it is their first time explaining it. We must listen as though it's the first time we've ever heard someone say, "I'm frustrated because I lost money" or "I am afraid I will run out of money in retirement." Ask them to tell you more about that. It's not fair to assume that we know what people want before we have listened to them.

For example, suppose you go to see a counselor. As soon as you walk into her office, with great intention and focus, she asks you how you are feeling. You tell her you feel sad. She looks you in the eye and in a kind and loving way says, "I see a lot of people who have to deal with sadness." And then she enthusiastically starts telling you about a new drug that has just been approved, and you could take it to fix your emotional trauma. She tells you all the benefits of the drug and the side effects, too.

As you sit there a bit dazed, you wait for her to finally take a breath so you can say, "I'm not here because of my emotional trauma. I'm here because my best friend just lost two children in a car accident. I feel very sad about it, but more importantly, I want to be able to know how to help her cope with her loss."

The counselor goes back to rattling on, "Oh, well, most of the people I talk to come in for depression because depression is one of the leading reasons why people see counselors today… anyway, our time is almost up. Would you like to schedule another appointment?"

And you will say, "OK, I appreciate that. Thank you for your time. I'll get back to you about setting another appointment. I need to think about it."

Somehow the counselor feels like she has contributed because she spent forty-five minutes pumping you full of "great information." Yet from an effectiveness standpoint, she did not serve your needs at all.

The counselor completely missed it.

And that's the last time you speak to her. It may sound ridiculous, but this exchange is often not far from reality with financial salespeople.

When you take time to listen and understand what others are saying, it ensures that your solution will be congruent with their specific, actual challenges and goals.

Intent Counts More Than Technique

Humans have an aura of intent. Subconsciously, we can feel the difference between someone who really cares about us and maybe stumbles a bit and someone who is really slick and just working their own agenda. It is difficult to achieve the highest level of success if you don't truly care about the individuals you serve. Seek first to understand and then to be understood. You may have heard the saying, "People don't care how much you know until they know how much you care." That is your *intent*—to care about the people you serve. And that starts the credibility journey.

Strive for Mutual Understanding, Not Mutual Mystification

The opposite of mutual understanding is "mutual mystification." With mystification, you believe you know what prospects need and want and what solution they will be pleased with and agree to but later find out you apparently missed something because the deal never closed. With mutual mystification, prospects feel like you don't quite get it. They may feel like you're treating them like everyone else, sense that you are not really listening to them, or feel a general lack of confidence that you are capable of performing well for them. The worst is that the meeting time seemed to go well, yet subconsciously they are not comfortable moving forward. This often results in the feared response of, "That's interesting. I'll have to think about it."

With *mutual understanding*, you hear what's being said, and you sense what's not being said (nonverbal communication). You recognize the discrepancies and changes in a saver's tone, pace of speech, and other nonverbal indication. Then you use that information to ask about the discrepancy in a polite and appropriate way. The purpose of doing this is to understand the client better and discover what's behind what you observe.

Beware—there are always competing voices in your mind:

1. One is the voice of the client (answering a question or telling you a story through verbal and nonverbal communication) that you can choose to pay attention to.

2. Another is the voice in your mind that's interpreting their words, filling in the blanks of incomplete information, hypothesizing about generalizations you've seen before, and preparing to ask the next question.
3. It may also be the voice that's preparing an argument for something the saver says that you feel you should defend for clarification (a jab in the face).
4. And you may have a discerning voice that says, "This is a sensitive topic. We need to get more history on this, but not yet...for now I need to just let them talk."

Knowing which voice you listen to and when will help determine the outcome of the relationship. This is applicable in all relationships, whether professional or personal. When you are talking with your spouse, your children, your friend, or your coworkers, be keenly aware of how completely or incompletely attentive you are to what they are saying and what you're doing in your mind. We owe it to our audience to be fully present and engaged.

Make it a goal in every interaction you have with savers to achieve a thorough understanding of exactly what is happening and exactly what savers are trying to say. You'll be amazed at how this can change your relationships. This is powerful stuff.

Concerned the Saver Is Talking to other Advisors?

Many advisors are concerned that a saver will be talking to other advisors. Instead of *wondering* if there is anyone else, simply ask the prospect during the interview. There is a specific way you can ask (in the ShiftMethods library) to determine what you are dealing with. When you ask the question the way we show you in the video, it helps you understand if the prospect is considering other alternatives ("I can do this myself" or "I need to talk to three other advisors" or "I'll probably just have my nephew implement this…") without encouraging him or her to seek other alternatives if they aren't already planning to.

Listening and understanding is our chief role as facilitators. When we do this well, it builds a foundation of mutual respect with everyone we meet. And it sets us apart from the average financial advisor. People will notice!

How Craig's Increased Self-Awareness Transformed His Practice

Craig is an advisor who was referred to me a while ago. He was very determined to grow. He worked twelve hours per day, six days per week. He equated effort with results, so he was intent on working, working, working, all the time. But as we discussed his daily regimen, he realized that he was so focused on "seeing more people" that he was giving off a subconscious vibe that he was always in a hurry and didn't really have time. Ironically, this could not have been further from the truth. He was very considerate and compassionate, but because of his hurried pace, he was misunderstood.

Often, we don't realize how we're coming across to prospects and clients. As an exercise, I ask advisors to imagine that there's a camera in the room, capturing them and their clients' behavior. Let's say we videotaped you with your client. Now you're watching that video play back on a monitor. You are watching yourself as a third party. As you are watching yourself, ask, "What's he thinking? What's he doing? Why is he sitting that way? What nonverbal communication is he sending?"

In this exercise, can you imagine how you are being received?

We did this to make Craig more aware of the image he was presenting subconsciously. He acted like he was in a hurry. He was trying to get through the fact finder as quickly as possible so he could gather information and then present a solution. He meant well, but what the clients were sensing is that he wasn't listening, that he was trying to sell them a product. It came across as though he was trying to pitch a solution and fix something they didn't necessarily ask him to fix.

He thought that he was doing the right thing by trying to see more people. What he realized is that *he couldn't even see the people who were sitting right in front of him.*

As a result of making it his intent to listen to clients and understand their concerns, needs, hopes, dreams, and fears, Craig just about doubled his production. Just one year into the ShiftMethods training, he had a little more than 100 percent growth. Plus, he was spending a little less time meeting with people. At that point, he was only one-third of the way through the training, so he has the potential for much more growth and refinement.

Shifting Your Methods

1. Being mindful of your end goal will significantly improve your chances of achieving it. Take a moment to write out your intent when you meet a new prospect:
    a. When I sit down with a new prospect, my intent is to _____.
    What else? _____
    _____

b. The most favorable outcome of our first meeting is the prospect thinking or saying _____.
   What else? _____

c. What can I do to benefit the saver in this meeting?
   _____
   What else? _____

2. Ask yourself these questions to gauge whether you are achieving mutual understanding or mutual mystification:
   a. Am I listening intently and attempting to understand the speaker's perspective (even if I don't agree)?
   b. Am I preparing a rebuttal?
   c. Am I hoping the saver will take a breath and be ready for the next question?
   d. Am I becoming annoyed with the saver, and am I catching myself starting to ignore what he or she is saying?
   e. Am I asking, "What else, what else, what else?" to reveal the *why* behind the *what*?

CHAPTER 6
How Top Producers Elevate and Grow Their Practices

Most advisors have successful practices and make good money. But they are working more hours than they would like, and they are spending more money than they want to. When they hear all the benefits they could enjoy by making a few strategic changes with ShiftMethods, they say, "It sounds too good to be true."

Most of the people who are referred to us are quite successful already. Still, it's not enough. In general, people who are successful don't take anything for granted. They're always looking to be better because they know the world is ever-changing. They know they need to adapt and adjust to be able to stay successful and to improve. There is a tension most people feel. They know they're good at what they do, but they also choose to insist on believing there must be something out there that could help them improve.

I recall my grandfather telling me many times, "You get what you are looking for. If you are looking for a solution, you will find a way to get it. If you believe you can't, you will find a way to prove your belief true."

Sometimes, advisors are reluctant to admit that they could be doing even better than they already are. A part of them doesn't want to be open to believing anything can help them achieve more than they ever dreamed because if they acknowledge it, then they must be open to change. This is not for you.

Ask yourself these questions: "Do I want to be better? Do I want to be my best?" If you are satisfied with where you are, think you are good enough, and don't need to get any better, then it is probably best that you give this book to a friend you think may want to be the best version of himself or herself. But if you say, "I want to be the best version of myself," then pay close attention—your world is changing right before your eyes.

Becoming more aware, more efficient, and better at the interview process makes you much more successful. Studies show that doing this will make you happier, more productive, and more efficient. And being open to getting better improves your ability to improve. You have two choices. You can be a serial salesperson who takes what comes your way, pretending like you're working hard at getting better, or you can be a serial winner. Serial winners have an innate need to continue to improve to continue to win. Every new level of success brings about new challenges, with an opportunity to rise to the occasion, improve your skills, fine-tune your abilities, and continue to progress.

Change Is Disruptive—But Rewarding

When there is something in the ShiftMethods library that seems contrary to or at odds with what you've done, ask yourself, "How is this different?" And if you were to implement it, how may it improve your practice?

Caution—humans tend to think and say things like, "That won't work in my situation because…" Protect your mind from that reflex response. Instead, think, "If I were to use that particular method, if it could improve my client interaction, how would it improve my client interaction?"

Here's an example that shows why this is important. Let's talk about inventions. Nearly every new creation is made by a diligent dreamer amid a constituency of nay-sayers. People love to say, "You can't do that!" or "It will never work" or "That will never happen" when we naively share our vision of the future. But something gnaws at us inside and inspires persistence to see the manifestation of what we are somehow inspired to believe to be true. We continue on, despite the crowd cheering against us, and now that very crowd and the world are better for it. When we persist, we are world changers.

Let's face it, change is disruptive, it is hard, and it is often not fun. But the fruit of diligently seeking a vision for a better way is how successful things like this great country are birthed. A small group of people were willing to forsake what modern science concluded was impossible. They got in a small boat with their families, taking the risk that potentially many in their group would not make it through the first winter in the new land. Yet we modernized folks have a challenging time opening our minds to a different method.

Hopefully you're laughing a little. It's not really funny, but laughter somehow breaks the tension of truth.

When I was growing up, I recall my grandfather asking me (every time he saw me), "What did you learn new today?" He waited until I responded, and then he would tell me what he learned. He passed away at the age of eighty-four, when I was twenty-six. Many years later, his question still burns in my mind daily: "What did you learn new today?"

One of our greatest opportunities toward fulfillment is learning every day.

How Don Increased His Revenue from $400,000 to $2.1 Million a Year

A gentleman named Don was referred to me for training. He was a very good producer, earning around $400,000 per year. He had a mechanical style. He was very deliberate in his approach, but his demeanor was a bit gruff. He was not very personable. He had played fullback on his small college football team, and like many successful people in this business, he was driven, driven, driven, like a dog with a bone. He would not stop. He would go after it and go after it and go after it.

He began ShiftMethods training long before it was in its current form, five years ago, and last year he earned $2.1 million. He went from $400,000 to $2.1 million. A big part of his transformation was a change in the way he saw himself. We discovered that he wasn't doing as good a job of listening as he could have been. He is intellectual and had a good knowledge of investments. All his clients loved him, but what was missing is that he wasn't being patient with the process of discovery. He was going on to the next thing, not realizing that his demeanor was giving off significant cues that were a bit offensive to some people. Those cues kept people from being willing to do business with him.

His heart's intention was to do the right thing. But he was missing opportunities with the people he was seeing because he was coming across as being impatient. His tenacity was keeping him from slowing down and being able to finish well what he started.

We discovered this by going through the process with him, looking at what he was doing, how many people he was seeing, and the discrepancy between those who loved him and those who were turned off by him.

I see that often—advisors are trying to do the right thing, but the people who are sitting with them don't feel that because the advisor is doing something else in his mind (it can appear as if he is almost daydreaming) rather than being present, he isn't as prepared for the meeting as he could be, and he's not as patient with the saver as he could be. The trouble with this approach is that you end up being super busy having lots of meetings (seeing lots of people) when you could be less busy, having fewer meetings, being more productive financially, and having a lot less to maintain—and of course, having more fun.

What's interesting is that Don had been in the business for twenty-one years, and I had been in the business for only five. He was old enough to be my father. Yet he was open to improving his strategies after twenty-one years in the business. He was at the top of his game, making $400,000.00 a year. Now he's making more than $2 million a year consistently.

Don was already at the top of his game when we met, and it took him four years to get to where he is now—at the *new* top of his game. So, even though what he did sounds simple, it took him four years to make many small adjustments. And he did it without seeing more people. In fact, now he has more free time to do other things. He serves as the assistant coach of his girls' soccer team two days a week and doesn't miss any games. This never would have been possible before he committed to improving his practice.

As Don's story demonstrates, ShiftMethods is a process. When Don first started embracing the program, he thought it was going to take a lot more time and that he would have to string out his client appointments. At first, it did feel like that. Soon, he experienced a much more direct, efficient, and fruitful exchange with his clients and prospects. He concluded, "The effectivity of communication is what launched my success. It's not something you can do, get it over with, and see results right away. It requires thinking about things in different ways and building repetition into your client interactions. When you do this consistently over time, you can elevate and grow your practice to levels you never imagined. And that is what I did."

Shifting Your Methods

1. To what extent are you raising the bar for your own level of success? When you achieve a goal, do you immediately set a new, even higher goal? What does the next level of success look like for you? Describe it, write it down, and list the steps for how you'll get there. What are the benefits you can enjoy if you rise to that new level of achievement?

2. What did you learn today? What did you learn yesterday? What do you want to learn tomorrow? Most people just take things as they come. Make it your goal to learn at least one new thing every day. Then, after a year, imagine how much you will have learned!
3. Envision your opportunities for improvement in effectivity.

CHAPTER 7
Nine Barriers to Avoid

We've talked about the strategies, characteristics, and behaviors that lead to phenomenal success because they differentiate ShiftMethods advisors from others. Now let's discuss barriers that can prevent you from achieving great success. They all relate to having a negative mind-set or attitude.

1. "I already know that"
The first barrier is having the attitude of "What are you going to tell me that I don't already know?"

I like to be very agreeable. It's pretty tough to be of benefit to someone who already knows everything. So here is my response to people who say this: "I'm probably going to tell you a lot of things you already know; however, I may say them in a way that you likely haven't put into practice before in your business."

Most importantly, the resulting effectivity will yield fruit you haven't known...*yet*!

2. "How are you any different?"

Sometimes people ask me, "How are you different from anyone else?"

My response is, "Effectivity—that's how it's different." And, you don't have to abandon your current methods to use ShiftMethods. It's much less disruptive to your process than most training programs. I will ask skeptical advisors to describe the types of training they've subjected themselves to in the past, what has been beneficial, what hasn't, what they have been able to use easily, the type of impact it has made, and how much they've invested in it. And then I will ask what they're looking for and describe how ShiftMethods can enhance what they're already doing.

Also, I share with them success stories, such as the one about Phil in the introduction, of people who were once skeptics but tried ShiftMethods and were astounded at their positive results. To elicit in skeptics the desire to expect positive results, I will ask them, "Are you the type of person who wants to believe that you can increase your business by fifty percent?" I want them to create the dream in their mind rather than telling them what they can accomplish. If you can believe it, it is possible, and it is only a matter of time before you do it.

If you don't believe it, it doesn't matter how many others have revolutionized their businesses...you won't join them.

3. "I want this to work immediately"

Another barrier to being open to improvement is wanting a quick fix. That's when advisors say, "Just tell me what to do. I'll do it, and I'll see results today or tomorrow."

My response to that is, "Little in life of sustaining value is a silver bullet." However, I did have one advisor who got approved for the courses on a Friday morning and invested more than four hours watching videos on the weekend. She said she attributed $39,100 in compensation the following week to things she learned in the videos. This is not normal. She was aggressive and determined.

If you want to be in better shape, you may look at your diet and exercise, but just because you change your perspective doesn't mean your health will improve. A catastrophic event such as a heart attack, stroke, or triple-bypass surgery may cause you to change your lifestyle habits, but it's not going to change your body immediately. To see sustainable evidence of positive change, it takes effort over time, like everything else.

4. "I really need this sale"
Some advisors feel pressure to make the sale because they need it to pay the bills. There is no bigger killer of a potential sale than a salesperson who seems under pressure. Under these circumstances, the harder you try, the more you "use the techniques," and the further you drive the prospect away. Prospects would never know how to tell you this, but they can sense subconsciously when you desperately need a sale. It makes them feel like prey, and they sense your predatory pressure to close. Relax, take some deep breaths, and ask yourself, "What is my goal? What is my intent in this interaction? To serve others...oh, yeah, that's right."

Get back on track, serve your clients by seeking to understand them, and have a great interview.

Listen well so you can better understand, which enables you to better serve. When you put yourself under pressure to close the deal, it is very hard to win. But when you put yourself under pressure to clearly understand and listen well to the prospect, it is yours to lose. Savers want guidance from professionals who care.

5. "I can convince this prospect"

"Watch this—I can convince this prospect to buy!" If you hear this statement playing in the back of your mind, and you are a hard worker, you will enjoy moderate success. But you will never be your very best. You will never consistently win the big cases or serve the best savers. You attract what you are. It's about listening to savers discuss what's important to them, understanding their needs, and being committed to being their partner as they meet those needs.

Don't focus on convincing anyone of anything. Channel your determined persistence into understanding. Use that great energy to seek to know the *why* behind the *what*. Focus on facilitating the best solution to a saver's financial situation.

6. "This won't work for me because…"

A big part of conquering performance plateaus is believing you can do much more than you ever dreamed. Having a "that won't work for me because…" mind-set is a "hard-stop" barrier to improvement. Believing you already know everything there is to know begins the downward spiral. Pride comes before the fall.

7. "My goal is to present the prospect with an impressive-looking plan"

Often, financial planning tends to be quite mathematical. You prepare material and present a plan, and a thick book shows every detail of savers' assets—where they started out, where they are going, and based on some assumptions, how their assets are projected to perform over time. When you present this material to the prospect, you've done all the homework, you are excited to show them your work, and it all makes sense logically, but what do they say? "Wow, you've done a lot of work. Thank you! You've given me a lot to think about. I will have to get back to you."

Even though you made the logical and appropriate recommendations, this prospect somehow doesn't have a good feeling about moving forward. Her response is a defensive one: "I need to think about it." This is a great example of the fruit of "mutual mystification." You firmly believe she will be back in the office to sign. She may even schedule another appointment.

On the other hand, when the prospect has a good feeling about the interaction, when she feels listened to, understood, and cared for, having a large, thorough, well-articulated bound financial planning document is unnecessary. It can create a false sense of security for you. You think, "It's all in the plan—how could anyone say no at this point?" But that is, in fact, what ends up happening way too often.

What you expected to be a close fizzles into a prospect whom you continue to "drip" and remain hopeful about.

You can have a well-articulated plan, but it is secondary to relational equity accumulated by caring, listening, and understanding. As fiduciaries, we know that every plan must adapt and adjust to changing life circumstances and changing market circumstances. So having an extravagant, detailed written plan is great for now. And when things change, the well-written plan will need to be modified.

8. "I'm not smart like you are"

Several years ago, a woman named Cynthia was referred to me for ShiftMethods training. She is very sharp, attractive, personable, and a really nice person. She was successful in the business and had been an advisor for five years. Her biggest hindrance was her mind-set—she didn't think she was capable of achieving at the levels of some of the top producers.

The barrier she faced was almost all related to how she saw herself. She knew the things she needed to do and was supposed to do, but because she didn't feel as comfortable, confident, or capable as others saw her, she wasn't producing at the level she was capable of. The solution was basically to facilitate her giving herself permission to be the best version of herself she could be.

The mentor who brought her into the business had a very strong personality and felt like he had to be the best, which created a glass ceiling above Cynthia—or at least that is how it felt for her. She didn't think she could rise to the level of her mentor, and she saw that as her limitation. What we uncovered is that she has a skill that goes way beyond the level of her mentor. She has exceeded even his level of success.

9. "Everything is fine the way it is"

Nothing in life is neutral. You are either sharpening your skills and improving, or you are slowly dulling your edge and becoming slightly more complacent.

You are either green and growing, or you are ripe and rotting.

Fight nature, and grow daily with the short and sweet, high-impact videos from ShiftMethods. Think differently!

• • •

As you can see, these destructive mind-sets benefit neither you nor prospects and clients. ShiftMethods training shows you a better way. As I study interactions between savers and financial professionals, I observe more and more that savers seek to have a feeling of trust, confidence, and goodwill about a financial professional more than anything else. Avoid destructive and negative behaviors, beliefs, and mind-sets, and be open to improving every interaction.

Shifting Your Methods

1. Review the barriers to success listed in this chapter. Have you said any of those things to yourself? Why? Next to each barrier/negative mind-set below, write "yes" or "no" to indicate if you have ever had these thoughts when working with clients or when presented with the potential for a different way of doing things:

Barrier/Negative Mind-Set	Have You Ever Thought This? (Answer Yes or No)
a. "I already know that"	_____
b. "How are you any different?"	_____
c. "I want this to work immediately"	_____
d. "I really need this sale"	_____
e. "I can convince this prospect"	_____
f. "This won't work for me because…"	_____
g. "My goal is to present the prospect with an impressive-looking plan"	_____
h. "I'm not smart like you are"	_____

2. If none of these barriers relate to you, are there others that do? What are they? How did you acquire them? What can we do to eliminate those barriers from your mind-set and life? How can you benefit by doing so?

CHAPTER 8
Thirteen Ways to Earn More Business in Less Time

The difference between the worst and best teams in baseball may appear to be insignificant in any given game.

Even the worst professional baseball teams win one-third of their games. And the very best baseball teams win only two-thirds of their games. Here is the false sense of security: if you are spending money on marketing, seeing people, and following a process, a decent number of people will buy your product. And if you are like most advisors, you feel a good level of success—after all, look at all the revenue you're generating. This business is amazing! Where else could you earn like this?

But…based on our experience, you are not nearly as productive or efficient as you are capable of being. And by using ShiftMethods, you will see yourself as being a lot better than what the scoreboard sometimes shows. You can have amateur skill accompanied with diligence and find decent success. Just like the worst team in baseball (not that any professional is anywhere near the worst, keep in mind, the worst baseball team is comprised of some of the greatest athletes in all of sports) still wins one-third of its games. Or you can develop professional skill, invest the same or less money in marketing, enjoy an elevated conversion rate, refine your process, and have a much larger number of your introductions call you "my advisor."

Using ShiftMethods training enables you to elevate and grow your practice to be more profitable—with less effort than you're accustomed to putting in. Let's look at thirteen ways the process can lead you to do that.

1. Know Your Numbers, But Don't Focus on Them

The more important it is to meet your numbers, the more important it is to focus on the client. Helping savers succeed is not only the key to being much more successful; it feels better. Don't be misled—helping savers get what they want is not charitable, selfless, or just an attempt to be kind. It is all of that and much, much more. It is a paradoxical means of getting what we want, and ironically, it is the best way for savers to get what they want. In a nutshell, if what we want is to serve the saver, then the saver will see our positive intentions and welcome our professional skill.

Intent plus expertise is what gives you the authority to have an influence. When clients feel that your intent is to serve them, they are much more likely to feel at ease and share vital information about their situation. And the better you understand your clients' wants, needs, and preferences, the better the likelihood you can bring the most appropriate solution strategy to the table. And the more likely they will embrace your guidance.

Often, the harder we try to sell, the more we fail. Focusing on the client's needs is where both parties win.

If you really want to meet your numbers, stop thinking about your numbers! Instead, start thinking about what clients need and how you can benefit them. You'll be amazed at how your numbers begin to improve because of what you're focusing on.

Changing focus = success. Shifting your methods = success.

2. Increase Your Case Size by 50 Percent

The typical salesperson is excited about his or her product. When you're a salesperson pitching a product, your prospects are generally thinking about what portion of their assets they want to put in that particular product. But when you change your role a little and instead take the role of a consultant who is giving them feedback on their *entire* plan and how it's aligned to give them the results they expect, then the conversation is about their *entire* portfolio—all their assets. At that point, you are operating from a point of strength for the saver because you know everything he or she has.

Let's say the Taylors come to me, and I'm doing the traditional "pitching them a product." They decide to put $200,000 of their assets with me. I may be pleased with that, yet all I know is that they have $200,000. But if I'm using ShiftMethods, and I'm giving them feedback on all their assets and how their plan is aligned with their goals, I will know they have a total of $1.5 million. Personally, I wouldn't take $200,000 from someone who has $1.5 million because investing that amount wouldn't make much of a difference proportionally in their bottom line. I wouldn't start with less than probably one-third of what they have—which is half a million dollars. And half a million dollars is already significantly more assets than the Taylors would have invested if I hadn't taken a consultative approach.

Timing is critical. It's important to discuss the value of the entire portfolio at the ideal time. If you ask clients what they have too early, they might hesitate to share. You have to have enough of what I call "relational equity." If you don't have enough relational equity, then once they tell you no, it sets a boundary that is tough to cross. We focus on timing a lot in the ShiftMethods library.

If you don't know all of what your prospects have, how are you ever going to help them with more than what they just offered you?

3. Increase Your Closing Ratio by 50 Percent

With ShiftMethods, we encourage advisors to get the focus off measuring the close and on *measuring the interaction.* In other words, don't keep looking at the scoreboard; keep focused on the process, and the scoreboard will light up. Shifting the focus from working toward closing a sale to working toward understanding prospects through a proper interview leaves the prospects much happier and the facilitator much happier and...you guessed it! A lot more, and bigger, "sales." ShiftMethods focuses on having a winning interaction.

However, in our business, we must measure our closing ratios to know how we're doing. So we do.

Your "closing ratio" is the number of people you meet vs. the number of people who become clients. For example, if you met fifty new people in a seminar series three months ago, how many of them are clients today? If you met a total of 392 new prospects last year, how many are clients today? If you are doing seminars and meeting twenty to thirty new people each month, how many of those are you closing? Ideally, you could be closing or getting referrals from 50 to 80 percent of your prospect introductions.

If you normally close 60 percent of your prospects, can you envision reaching a closing rate of 80 percent consistently over the next three years? If you normally close 80 percent, can you envision closing 90 percent consistently over the next three years? Think about it—the same marketing expense, the same number of new prospects seen, the same time invested, but with a marginal increase in closing. This directly translates into more profit and more referrals, which results in much greater efficiency.

Just about every advisor has a certain level of suspicion and, depending on his or her own experiences, appropriate level of cynicism. Similarly, just about every saver has a certain level of suspicion and cynicism, but if savers are sitting with you to discuss their finances, then it's reasonable to expect that they will disclose their assets to you. After all, it is what they are there for.

It's like going to the doctor. He will enter the examination room and ask you, "So what brings you in today? What types of symptoms are you having?" You will give him a detailed answer because that's why you are there. You made an appointment to benefit from the professional service he provides. But if that doctor has a horrible bedside manner, you might hesitate before answering because you feel uneasy and already are skeptical of any forthcoming diagnosis.

4. Acknowledge That a 100 Percent Closing Ratio Isn't Realistic

Some prospects have no intention of becoming your clients. So it's a very appropriate concern that a prospect may want to talk to you for the sole reason of kicking the tires and has no intention of becoming a client. When you see there is nothing left to do but initiate the close, the prospect feels like a shopper. And what do shoppers do? That's right—they shop and shop and shop. Sometimes they make a purchase, and sometimes they just think about it.

Sometimes, "losing the sale" is a natural response to a proper interview. Let's face it, our solutions are not for everyone. The only way we know if our solutions are appropriate for the prospects sitting beside us is to go through a proper interview and determine three things:

1. If they have three to five needs
2. If they would like our help
3. If they see that we can benefit them financially

We've met a number of do-it-yourselfers who have things well under control. They have significant discretionary assets, and they do not need a financial professional. When you serve these do-it-yourselfers well, they often turn out to be great resources for referrals. When you impress the do-it-yourselfer who impresses others, you get referrals because everyone knows they are sharp and values their recommendation.

They know when you've given it to them straight and you've been a benefit to them. They see that you're doing the right thing. When they see that, they want to help people they know by referring them to you.

They want to help others by referring them to you!

Isn't that exactly what you want?

You're not going to get business from prospects who are determined to do it themselves anyway. If you can't get more business, get more friends. More friends = more referrals, and more referrals = more clients—and friends.

If you have a great product to sell, and you are not a great listener, you will attract shoppers who see your "great product" as a commodity they need to compare to others. You will make a good living with this approach if you see a lot of people, but you will never fully develop your skill to be a master craftsman in the art of true salesmanship.

An unfortunate tragedy—never fully developing your skill to be a master craftsman.

And you know what? It doesn't have to be that way!

5. Avoid the Polarity Response

When people feel pushed or manipulated, they often respond abruptly by moving aggressively in the opposite direction. Once this has happened, it's nearly impossible to close the sale. You may represent the best products and present the best solution, and even be the best listener, but if a client feels you are being inappropriate, he or she will subconsciously run. Here's the tragedy: they may still be sitting with you. Or, even worse, they may set up another meeting, but folks, "Elvis has left the building." When the manipulation button is tripped, a subconscious separation begins. Only luck will make them clients of yours. Even if you do sign some business with them, in the long run, they probably won't be clients you will want to serve because of the foundation you laid.

Conversely, when using ShiftMethods, you set the tone early in the first introduction for a thriving saver–facilitator relationship. Every move you make will further affirm your reputation and the expectation that has been set. Your clients will greatly value your expertise and methods—*and* they will want to share you with others.

6. Don't Fall for the Façade of Seeing More People

We jokingly refer to this as "shiny object management." Marketing companies are tripping over each other to present you with the latest shiny object, touted as the trick to attract more prospects so you can "see more people." Most advisors we meet are busy enough. They don't need to pack more into the already super busy week by "seeing more people."

At ShiftMethods, we believe the key to success is seeing the same amount of people or fewer while making every move count. Imagine that baseball team we talked about earlier needing to win the same number of games as the first-place team, and they couldn't end the season until they did so. The normal season is 162 games and lasts six months. Imagine the lower-placed teams needing to play eleven months to get enough wins (closes) before they could rest until the next season! It sounds ridiculous, but many advisors are burning the candle at both ends trying to see enough people to get enough closes so they can meet goals. And guess what? It doesn't have to be that way!

Studies show that 65 percent of salespeople are pursuing prospects who will not do business with them. What a waste of time! What if you could have a better idea whether a prospect was going to be a client earlier on in the game and know if you should continue to pursue the client? What if you could transform a few of the maybes each month to closes? That would significantly improve your bottom line. You are seeing them anyway; you might as well close them.

I hear many professionals and wholesalers state that seeing more people is the solution. That could not be further from the truth.

The key to success is *seeing the people sitting in front of you and having better interactions with them.*

Seeing more people only makes you busier, more stressed, and less able to give full attention to the person who is sitting in front of you.

7. Know Who the Biggest Loser Is

When you meet new prospects and you know there is significant benefit you and your firm could provide, yet for whatever reason, they do not become clients, who loses? Here is a shift in the typical mind-set—the prospect is the biggest loser. Here's why. You have an endless supply of prospects who want to sit with you to get feedback on what they have and how their assets are aligned to get the results they expect. At the end of the day, you will go home to your family and do what you normally do, and they will go on with their saving and investing career doing what they normally do. But then one of those typical yet unforeseen market or economic events happens, and it results in the saver being disappointed, frustrated, and even worse, discouraged enough to lose hope that they can get what they expect with their retirement assets. That's a tough situation.

When you miss the opportunity to serve the saver, the biggest loser is the saver, but you know what? It doesn't have to be that way!

Our advisors find, using ShiftMethods, that there are significantly fewer situations in which the prospect loses. When you have a proper interview, it is nearly a foregone conclusion you will be in a position to give nearly everyone you sit with proper feedback on how what they have is aligned to likely give them what they expect.

8. Value the Prospect Who Says No

This is counterintuitive and powerful, but we almost encourage the client to say no! Why? We want to make it clear to the prospect, out of respect, that it is their money, and we would never sit in the place of presumption to tell them what they should do with their life savings.

Having a few good "no" responses in the dialogue makes for great interactions that lead to understanding—and great clients. It shows you are engaged with them in a productive and forthright conversation. Encourage them to get the no's out early in the conversation. This allows them to set parameters for the discussion and lets you know their biases toward certain topics or ideas. This approach opens people to ideas and methods that may be beneficial to them that they otherwise may not have considered.

This is how it works. When you tell someone, "Hey, you should do this...," what do you suppose their reflex response is? You guessed it: "I don't need to do that. I'm all set." Conversely, when you present a concept in a way that enables clients to envision themselves seeing the benefit of the concept, it opens their minds to consider the possibility. An important step toward positive change is simply considering the possibility.

It's just like you, reading this book right now. Things are happening in your mind. You are opening yourself to consider the idea of improving your client interaction (even if you are the best you know). As you open your mind to consider the possibility, you open yourself to the possibility of positive change. As you open yourself, positive things just start to happen.

9. Imagine for a Moment (Warning—Graphic Content)

Imagine this—what if the roles were reversed? What if it were your "financial pants" that were being pulled down, and you were the one being exposed to everyone sitting in the room? It's important to be aware of how it must feel for them and have empathy toward your prospects and clients because they're bringing their successes, failures, challenges, embarrassments, and frustrations to you. Their very private financial lives are being exposed to you. It is critical to handle that in a way that makes them comfortable.

10. Spend 50 Percent Less Time in the Office

When you use ShiftMethods and your case size increases, then you won't need to invest as much in marketing to create the same amount of business as you can get through improved effectivity and referrals.

GEORGE WELLS

When I started out as a financial advisor, I did seminars to get new clients. After a few years in the business, I chose to stop doing seminars and focused on having 100 percent of my business come from referrals. So, rather than going out to meet fifty new people every month and spending time trying to close a few sales, I would meet five or six new referrals and close the same number of people every month.

The referrals I am meeting with want to meet with me. They are seeking me out to get my feedback on what they have and how it is aligned to get what they expect. I have a reputation of doing this in a manner that gives them an experience that exceeds their expectations, based on the experiences they have heard about from people they know and trust.

Now, many of the people who are referred to us aren't necessarily looking for a new advisor. In fact, two-thirds of them are not looking for a new advisor. They feel like they're all set. They feel like they're tended to very well. They may be do-it-yourselfers. Or maybe their financial professional is a great friend of theirs. But because they've heard so much about us, they want to meet with us and get our thoughts on what they're doing to see if they're missing anything important.

So they'll come in and say, "I don't want to waste your time, but my friend, John, speaks very highly of you, and I just want to see what you think about what I'm doing. I have a couple of questions. I want to tell you I really like my advisor. I've known him for a long, long time. He's a great friend of mine. But nevertheless, my friend, John, speaks very highly of you, and I want to see if there's something I am missing."

11. Transform Your Business into 100 Percent Referrals

Typically, when you ask for referrals, the client will say, "I don't know of anyone who has asked me to refer them to a financial person." But with ShiftMethods, you will get referrals from people who have not asked to be referred to an advisor. Your clients will be such raving fans about the experience they've had with you that they will want others to be able to have the same experience. They will tell the people they know, "I know you feel like you're all set. I know you like your financial person. But you've got to talk to my person. Wait till you see what they say. Wait till you have this experience with them. They do all this stuff that I've never experienced before. You've got to talk to him."

Then referrals just call our office out of the blue. They'll say something like, "I feel like I'm all set. I feel like I'm well-tended-to. Nevertheless, Mr. and Mrs. Jones say we should meet with you and see if something is missing. We don't want to waste your time, but they said you'd be happy to meet with us and that you want us to have an experience that exceeds our expectation. So what do I do now?" And then they schedule an appointment.

These are people who are not looking for an advisor. They are just excited because our clients are so excited with the experience they've had, they're telling others about it. They want them to experience it as well.

The reason people call us based on the experiences others have had with us, even if they think they're all set, is because of two powerful forces at work: Fear of Missing Out (FOMO) and approachability.

- **FOMO**—From the beginning of time, fear of danger has kept us alive. Today that fear also comes in the form of FOMO—Fear of Missing Out. No one wants to miss out on something they could be doing better. From the beginning of time, curiosity has been a great motivator as well. People have an inherent hope that something better exists. In addition, people have an inherent fear that something bad is going to happen and potentially leave them disappointed. This is why even those who would say they are "all set" appreciate our interview process because we give them feedback on what they have, how it is aligned to give them what they expect, and how it is positioned to avoid regret.
- **Approachability**—I believe a big deterrent in introductions is fear that the financial person is going to try to "sell them something." With ShiftMethods, savers don't feel like they need to keep their guard up. They know exactly what will happen and exactly what will not happen.

Referrals are inevitable when the product or service is extraordinary.

It's like you just got the new smartphone, and you know someone else who got a new phone just six months ago. You can't help but say to her, "Man, this phone is awesome."

She says, "I don't need a phone."

And you say, "Well, yeah, that's fine. I'm just telling you, the phone I've got is unbelievable."

So she asks you to tell her more about the phone you have. You say, "Well, it has this, and it does this and this...it used to not be able to do this, but now it does this, and it doesn't have this problem that I had before."

She starts thinking, "Well, shoot, I just got my phone six months ago, but maybe I'll check that out."

And then because of your enthusiasm and experience, she asks you, "Where can I check out that phone?"

This is the type of emotional exchange that initiates referrals seeking us out.

When you use the ShiftMethods approach, people who trust and value you will refer other people to you over and over again. You will no longer have to spend your time, effort, and resources looking for clients. And the people who are referred to you will come to you already excited to meet you and engage in your process.

Our clients refer people to us who haven't approached them to say they are looking for financial assistance. Let's put ourselves in their position. If you are the saver, you believe (hope, *want* to believe) you have a plan that fits well with your objectives. If a well-respected professional agrees and compliments you for it, that makes you feel affirmed and good...that is what the saver expects from us, and that is what we do.

12. Compliment What They've Done
No matter how good a financial plan you've created for a client is, it is unlikely that any other financial advisor is looking at that

plan and complimenting the client on it. If you are reviewing a great financial plan another advisor has created, compliment the client on it! This is a way to win every time. Remember, it is our objective (bias) for the prospect or client to have an experience while meeting and working with us that exceeds their expectations. If they have a great plan, don't be bashful to tell them that. As you would presumably expect, however, even the best plans will have some areas where improvements can be made. Politely giving this feedback allows the saver to be in control.

Having our clients insist on referring others to meet with us is something that sets us apart in the industry. Rather than being afraid of giving up a list of names or exposing their inner circle of friends, our clients are excited to invite others to extend our expertise. With traditional methods, those who are referring or being referred fear that the salesperson will "talk them into" something they may later regret, so they never take the introduction. It is easier to do nothing than to expose themselves to another possible mistake. In addition, many salespeople are inappropriately aggressive, and it may feel like that "predator vs. prey" model.

13. Dominate Your Profession

The World Series winning baseball team still doesn't win every game, but its players do get the World Series rings because they play every moment of every game well, execute every play in the most effective and efficient way to minimize errors, score runs, and enjoy the highest probability of success. Not too shabby. And one of our favorite parts about winning in the financial business is that you and your clients will not only get what you expect, you have a lot more fun. Every interaction will end better than it started. You will be less frustrated because more of the clients you should have won will be the clients you did win. And when it doesn't work out with a prospect, you can know that in the long run, it is probably much better that way.

Using ShiftMethods, it is nearly certain that you will have the privilege of being an invaluable resource to your clients and referrals. And when you do that, you will elevate and grow your practice in a way that seems effortless (even though we both know success is no accident).

Shifting Your Methods

1. To what extent do you focus on your closing ratio? Focus instead on the quality of interaction with your clients.
2. To what extent do you act as a consultant who is giving your prospects and clients feedback on their *entire* plan and how it's aligned to give them the results they expect? Start focusing the conversation on *all* their assets, and you can increase your case size.
3. What percentage of your current book of business came from referrals? Consider using ShiftMethods to get to 100 percent referrals. Think of how much time, money, and effort you could save if you spent your time meeting with referred clients instead of chasing after new clients!
4. What are your thoughts about FOMO and approachability motivators?

CHAPTER 9
The Seven Tenets of ShiftMethods

Now that you know about the philosophy behind ShiftMethods, and you've read about how it can make a significant difference in your practice while supplementing what you're already doing, let's look at the overall ShiftMethods approach.

The diagram on the next page is a visual representation of the seven tenets that compose the ShiftMethods process. Let's look at each of these key components in more detail.

1. Flexible Bridge

ShiftMethods encourages you to keep doing what's working. Don't abandon the processes that are bringing you positive results. ShiftMethods meets you where you are, sprinkling in effective strategies and processes to your already-great processes day by day.

GEORGE WELLS

Flexible Bridge
Don't abandon what is working! ShiftMethods meets you where you are. Add what's great to your current process by sprinkling it in day by day.

Timeless Benefits
Every new marketing strategy ultimately needs to be replaced. The ShiftMethods education is a seed of knowledge that produces lifetime fruit.

Simple Steps
Every topic is broken down into direct how and why in 1-2 minute video bites. Most prefer to watch on their smart device for convenience.

You're the Hero
We find today's financial professionals to hold a much more significant role in society than is often portrayed. You are much better at what you do than the media and sometimes the clients reflect. Unleash the hero in you as you begin to think differently. Transform your client experiences with the ShiftMethods.

Evergreen Material
Although many of the techniques and strategies are timeless, new content is always being added based on feedback and 'what if ..?' scenarios.

Easy
Receive daily text messages on topics of interest. 24/7 library access through your preferred device. Feedback loop to ensure your experience is most beneficial.

Daily Compound Effect
Over the next three years your life will change for the better day by day, step by step. All you have to do is watch the video and ponder how ShiftMethods compares to your practices.

You take a huge risk when you change what you've been doing because as you stop doing what you know and start doing something new, you're in limbo for a while, in no man's land. This can be very uncomfortable because you're changing what you've done in the past, and it takes time for the new processes to become familiar and habitual.

THINK DIFFERENTLY

With ShiftMethods, you keep everything you're doing well and add new strategies as you're comfortable. ShiftMethods is a flexible bridge between what you're doing now and what you will evolve to be doing in the future.

The way you start to add in something new is by thinking about it. All you need to do is be aware of the new idea and think about it. Your daily habits will begin to change just because you're exposing yourself to some different thought. You don't have to *try* to change; you will begin to change just by thinking about doing things from a different perspective. Think, "If I did that, how would it look?" In your meetings, you'll notice that you will start to say things in a different way. You'll start to operate in a different way. And of course, you'll start to see different results.

2. Timeless Benefits

In the financial services business, much of what we do has a "shelf life" and requires replacement. Typical marketing always needs to be replaced because marketing tactics grow old. There is a perpetual need to do marketing to get in front of new people, whether that means buying leads, hosting seminars, or figuring out some other gimmick to get a prospect's attention. Things are always changing, so we always need to replace our marketing strategies for getting in front of new people. With ShiftMethods training, once you learn new skills, you won't have to replace them. Like any skill, once you learn it, you'll always know it. When you learn how to ride a bicycle, you never need to learn how to ride a bike again.

Now, if you want to enter bike races and perform at a high level, you will need to learn more advanced cycling techniques, beyond the basics.

So, instead of searching for more ways of spending money on marketing to see more people, work on improving your skills and your client interactions. That will make you better at what you do, and you will have that education for the rest of your life that does not need to be replaced.

My grandfather said, "Your education is something no one can ever take away." You can lose your health, your job, and your car but you cannot lose your experience or your education. And, as mentioned earlier, he also said, "You can't learn it any younger." The sooner you can learn new things, the sooner you can benefit from them for the rest of your life. ShiftMethods training is a timeless benefit.

3. Simple Steps
ShiftMethods training is broken down into one- to two-minute video bites. That makes it simple to learn, digest, and use specific concepts and strategies.

I've attended seminars that lasted a day and a half, and someone talked for six hours the first day and four hours the next day. Those ten hours of exposure might be reduced to twenty-three ShiftMethods videos that total thirty-four minutes of material. With traditional training, we receive more information than we can ever use, and then we forget it. The nuggets of useful information are buried in those long presentations, with breaks in between, and we end up forgetting most of what we hear.

Even if you write the key points down, you might end up with twelve pages of notes, with maybe five to seven key ideas that you pull out of that day and a half. Our ShiftMethods videos condense those ten hours of meetings into a manageable number of brief video clips. You can watch those videos on specific topics and be reminded of the critical concepts you learned over and over again, easily, so you're actually able to apply the strategies and improve your skills.

People in some organizations boast about having more than one thousand hours of training. Well, the reality of it is, if you have access to over one thousand hours of training, when are you going to go through it? And if my client appointments last for an hour each, what am I applying? Can someone tell me what's applicable and what's not?

We break important training concepts into simple steps. We tell you what's applicable to your business and why it's applicable. We explain how to use a concept and describe the effect you should expect in your interactions with your clients.

4. Your Role as a Hero
Here are three facts that I hope will encourage you:

1. You are way better than you see yourself.
2. You are way better than your clients see you.
3. Awareness of this will instigate improvement.

You care about your clients, just like you care about your own family. You're in this business because you like taking care of people, figuring out how to align their resources with what's important to them, and easing their fear of regret.

Often, our fear of clients' distrust and mistrust occupies space in our minds and derails us from being what we are called to be—a hero to our clients, financially. You are their facilitator, the one who helps them align what they have with what's most important to them. That is a heroic calling because if people are worried about money, it means they can't accomplish what's important to them, whether it's being able to afford medical treatments, having memorable experiences, or taking a break from work to spend time with their families. They often fear that if something goes wrong, they could lose, and that fear can be paralyzing.

As a financial advisor, you hold the key to peace in people's minds. You lead them to a discovery that not only accomplishes their objectives from a performance standpoint but gives them peace of mind so that they can be comfortable with fluctuations in the market and in their own accounts. We have the privilege of being able to serve people, and that is a very high calling. ShiftMethods makes it easier for you and your clients to see the hero inside of you.

5. Evergreen Material

So many of the concepts are timeless, and we are constantly adding techniques and strategies to the ShiftMethods library—the material is evergreen (always growing). Based on feedback from you, and many others who have gone before you, we continue to create content that is applicable today. Also, our library is continually adapting. The core principles of ShiftMethods do not change, but what does change is the application of those principles in the constantly changing environment.

For example, right now we are wondering what will happen with the fiduciary rule and how it will affect an advisor's practice.

We spend a lot of time talking about it, but maybe when we look back on it three years from now, we will see that the change for advisors was minimal. A new rule might seem disruptive, but our number one role—which is to understand clients, listen to them, and align what they have with what's most important to them—will not change.

The procedural details about disclosing fees might change, but the core basis of what we do will not change. Our evergreen material addresses changes in our environment that affect how we interact with our clients. Our content keeps you relevant.

6. Easy Access
It's easy to access ShiftMethods videos. You will receive daily text messages on topics of interest, and you'll get 24/7 access to our library of videos.

You can learn during those little holes you have in your day, whether you're standing in line at the grocery store or waiting for your lunch. You can watch brief video clips as reminders or as inspiration. You'll receive the videos in a way that's convenient for you, so they are easy to use.

7. Daily Compound Effect
Anything you want to be better at takes time. You cannot hit fast-forward on time and practice. No one hits the pinnacle of success with a quick fix. Yet we often focus intensely on something for a moment, and then we move on to the next thing. If you can disrupt human nature and commit yourself to small bites of a large goal, over time, you will see great success, compounded daily.

With ShiftMethods, over the next few years of your life, you will change for the better, day by day, step by step. And all you have to do is watch a video and ponder how ShiftMethods compares to your practice.

Anyone who wants to get in great physical shape cannot do it overnight. Anyone who wants to make better health choices cannot do it overnight. Anyone who wants to become the best athlete or the best musician, no matter how skilled you are, must work at improving over time. Nothing happens overnight. Small improvements you make each day have a compounding effect over time. It's the daily compound effect.

For example, if you reduce your daily consumption by just 100 calories, you will lose 10 pounds in a year. One cup of skim milk contains 100 calories. You'll never miss the extra 100 calories each day, but in a year, you will be missing 10 pounds. ShiftMethods makes small changes every day. So over a year's time—day by day—you will see significant, noticeable results. Now, you could starve yourself for thirty days and lose ten pounds, but it will be more comfortable, and the results will be more sustainable, if you take in 100 fewer calories every day for a year.

Step by step, the benefits accumulate. Small changes made over the long term are more likely to result in big improvements than big changes made all at once.

A great example is the Fitbit®, a wireless-enabled fitness tracker that you wear to monitor your activity level and vital signs. Let's say you decide to participate in a Fitbit challenge, and the goal is for everyone to take 10,000 steps in one day. And you start as an average person who normally does about 4,000 steps per day.

So that first day, you're really excited about making the goal, and you go on several walks and get to 10,000 steps. The next day, you're super excited, and you do 8,000. The next day, you do 7,000, and the fourth day, you do 4,000. Then a few days after that, you feel so guilty that you take your Fitbit off your hand, and it sits on a shelf.

That's what happens when you try to make big changes too fast. If you had taken a longer-term approach, you likely will have more success. Recognizing that you typically take 4,000 steps per day, you decide to take 5,000 steps per day and commit to leave the Fitbit on for the next 60 days, even if you don't meet your daily goals. Your potential for stick-to-itiveness is going to be significantly better.

This story is what happened to me. I bought a Fitbit in May 2016, and for ten days, I was super-duper excited about it. Yet, after 17 days, I took it off and didn't put it on again until October. I wore it for four days and was moderately excited about it but felt that I wasn't going to be able to follow through, so I took it off. Then, in January 2017, I put it on and decided to do nothing for 60 days but monitor what I was doing. I didn't even want to do that because of all the guilt I felt about my two previous experiences, but I put it on anyway.

Then some people I know started bugging me about doing a competition, so I did. My competitive nature kicked in, and I couldn't help myself. The first week, I was really competitive but lost the competition. It was just too many steps for me to take in a day. So the next week, I decided to take a slower approach and make a little progress consistently over time. By the end of May 2017, I was still wearing my Fitbit. I lost the twenty pounds I wanted to lose in only eight weeks, and I have maintained my lower weight.

To achieve the daily compound effect, I had to pace myself and lose an appropriate amount of weight, about one pound every three days.

We have to realize that we're not going to accomplish big changes in one day, one week, or even one month. As we commit ourselves to small bites of change, we see massive change over time.

When we try to do too much too soon, we feel guilty and embarrassed that we didn't achieve those too-ambitious goals. So we have to start out with the expectation that we will make small changes consistently, over time. We monitor what we're doing and improve a little bit at a time. And then, all of a sudden, something clicks, and we start seeing results.

That's the ShiftMethods way. Just think about it. If you're putting something new in front of you, thinking about it, and exposing yourself to new ideas, the way you do things will change. Something will change, and you will see progress. It has to happen. You cannot have exposure without an effect. You cannot un-ring the bell.

This concept of the daily compound effect loops us back to where we began, at the "flexible bridge"—the gradual acceptance of new material that supplements what you're currently doing that works for you.

If you are like many, this book has already been a catalyst to reap small benefits of a slight shift in the way you interact with clients. Even small changes in mind-set and procedure lead to significant results over time.

Commencement
You Deserve the Best

This is where we begin. You invested the time to read through this book. Thank *you* for that, by the way, and thank *the one* who referred you. You paused and reflected at the appropriate times to think about how ShiftMethods will change your life, your business—anything you're thinking about changing.

The next choice is the most important decision: What are you going to do next? You're probably not like most people because you are reading the end of this book.

Most people don't finish things.

To finish this, however, is to *commence*—to begin the process of transformation in your own practice, to begin the journey to see the impact of ShiftMethods that we've only spoken of in this book.

Obviously, you have done a lot of things successfully over the years to get to where you are today. We're excited for you and for all the opportunity that awaits as you further engage yourself to become the best version of yourself as you think differently.

Individual advisors, go to www.shiftmethods.com/advisor for more insights.

About the Author and ShiftMethods

After being raised on a farm in the Midwest, George Wells began using his modest upbringing and engineering training to create innovative processes to bring clarity and easy-to-understand effectivity methods to corporate, professional and individual clients.

• • •

ShiftMethods is effectivity training. Each video covers a specific topic succinctly. Simple, direct methods allow review of key concepts again and again, efficiently.

For corporate clients, after establishing a value proposition relative to needs and objectives, ShiftMethods conducts a beta test proof of concept of effectivity. ShiftMethods assumes responsibility for the user adaption rate, the efficacy, and the value proposition created. Instead of selling companies an off-the-shelf tool, ShiftMethods develops a process that will lead to improvements in the bottom line ensuring effectivity.

ShiftMethods builds white-label product for companies using their own acronyms and their current processes. They deliver strategies that are tailored for their unique situations, guiding them through the steps they need to follow to improve effectivity without disruption. The videos are the accumulation of experience working with others on skills that have now improved.

For more, go to www.shiftmethods.com/corporate.

• • •

A few years ago, I was interviewed by a journalist. Follow the link below to get details from that interview, along with additional information about how my formative years set the stage for my career in financial services—and the creation of ShiftMethods.

www.shiftmethods.com/InterviewGeorge

www.ingramcontent.com/pod-product-compliance
Lightning Source LLC
Chambersburg PA
CBHW071548240526
45470CB00023B/1638